Wyoming
CURIOSITIES

QUIRKY CHARACTERS, ROADSIDE ODDITIES & OTHER OFFBEAT STUFF

DINA MISHEV

Uncle Gus —

You probably won't randomly see this
on a Northwest Airlines flight! See you
soon.

Love,

Dave

INSIDERS' G

GUILFORD, CONNE

AN IMPRINT OF THE GLOBE

D1010157

The prices, rates, and hours listed in this guidebook were confirmed at press time. We recommend, however, that you call establishments to obtain current information before traveling.

To buy books in quantity for corporate use or incentives, call **(800) 962–0973** or e-mail **premiums@GlobePequot.com.**

INSIDERS' GUIDE®

Text design by Nancy Freeborn
Layout by Debbie Nicolais
Maps created by Rusty Nelson © Morris Book Publishing, LLC
Photo credits: p. 4 Melody Roberts; p. 9 Sweetwater County Museum; p. 29 Debora Soulé/Community Fine Arts Center; p. 32 Courtesy Sweetwater County Historical Museum; pp. 37, 40, 56, 262 Brian Harder; p. 52 Sean Campbell; p. 72 Greta Gretzinger; p. 83 Jackson Hole Mountain Resort; p. 84 Becky Eidemiller; pp. 116, 117 U.S. Bureau of Land Management, Lander Field Office; p. 120, 175 Wyoming Travel & Tourism; pp. 121, 122 Tana Libolt; p.124 Richard Collier/Wyoming Department of State Parks & Cultural Resources; p. 142 Lee Bender; pp. 158, 165 Cheyenne Area Convention and Visitors Bureau; p. 172 Marvin Cronberg; p. 185 UW Athletics Media Relations; 187 UW Photo; p. 190 Courtesy of the Wyoming Territorial Prison State Historic Site; p. 192 Bob Johnson, V.P. Operations; p. 201 The Wagner Perspective; p. 205 Jo Ann B. Davis; p. 209 William Sheehan, owner; p. 221 Karen Barlow/Campbell County Rockpile Museum; p. 236 DeeDee Tays Johnson; p. 239 Dana Prater; p. 254 Worland-Ten Sleep Chamber of Commerce; p. 256 Michael B. Willard. All other photos are by the author.

Library of Congress Cataloging-in-Publication Data is available.
ISBN: 978-0-7627-4365-0

Manufactured in the United States of America
First Edition/First Printing

For my parents, who taught me the joy of traveling . . . and that every vista and oddity encountered along the way was worth at least a few moments' stop and oftentimes an entire day of exploration.

WYOMING

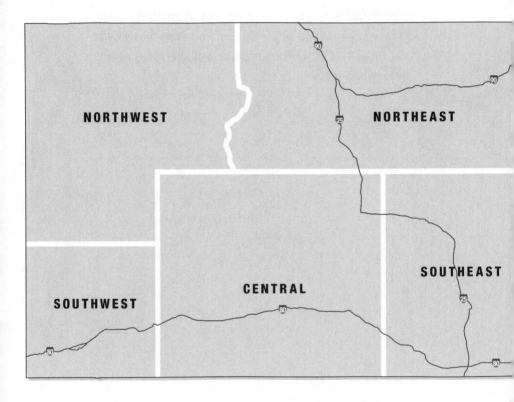

Contents

Acknowledgments

Populationwise, Wyoming is so small that I wouldn't be too far off base thanking each and every resident in the state. Over the months it took me to write this book, it seems there are few friends, friends of friends, chambers of commerce, ranchers, geologists, museum curators, gas station attendants, artists, guides, and fellow writers whose brains I did not pick and whose fingers I did not trouble to snap a photo or two. So, thanks to everyone who helped with this book in any way.

Several people, however, do deserve specific mention. Elaina Oliver taught me enough about Yellowstone to fill several books. Both Darren Rudloff and Rick Ammon at the Cheyenne Area Convention and Visitors Bureau know their corner of the state inside and out and then some. Wyoming Travel and Tourism is responsible for many of the photos (not to mention getting me this job in the first place). More personally, thanks to Brian "SG" Harder for allowing me to almost completely disappear into my office for much longer than I initially expected, for making sure I didn't starve, and for keeping me laughing. Carol Viau kept me focused on the light at the end of the tunnel. As I have said since my first-ever real writing assignment (that'd be a paper on the U.S. Constitution for a high school history class), thanks to my mom for being the best proofreader, research assistant, and photo editor available. Without her, I would have missed my deadline by even more and perhaps never discovered pygmy demons. Without MM I would have missed out on even more important things than pygmy demons (yes, although unbelievable, there are more important things than pygmy demons). And of course, thanks too to my dad, not only for lending me Mom, but also for supporting all my crazy ideas over the years. Lastly, thanks to my editor Mike, who took in stride the curveballs I threw him.

I should also take this opportunity to apologize to everyone subjected to my limited and usually inappropriate topics of conversation—

two-bodied sheep, tourist-ready gas chambers, human shoes—at various social engagements over the past several months. Really, though, can you blame a girl for getting excited about this stuff?

Introduction

I wasn't lucky enough to be born in Wyoming . . . or even in the same time zone. I'm a native of the Old Line State (that's Maryland for those not up on nicknames), and, after graduating from a big-city college, I liked the idea of living in the least populated state in the country. And if one of the few other people in that state just happened to be actor Harrison Ford, all the better.

I had been to Jackson Hole only once—in seventh grade while on a cross-country driving vacation with my family—but the memories were vivid: mountains, cowboys, mountains, fighting in the back seat of my parents' Oldsmobile with my younger brother, skies so wide and blue I took pictures of them, mountains, and wild animals whose only East Coast appearance was in zoos. When looking to relocate to Wyoming, I zeroed in on Jackson Hole because of these memories (mountains) and because it is home to some of the most challenging ski slopes in the country. I couldn't really ski at the time. Nonetheless, I liked the idea of being a ski bum as much as I liked the idea of living in a state in which wild animals far outnumber people and where towns' elevations routinely exceed their populations. So it was off to Jackson Hole, with my math and economics degrees in hand. I made the drive west on Interstate 80 with my mom, a Jeep Cherokee that needed two quarts of oil every 100 miles, and the promise of a rented room in the home of someone who made a point of asking during our roommate interview whether I was fine with game meat curing in the kitchen.

The move was supposed to be a temporary one—a Boston law

school had extended me an offer of admission and then allowed me to defer it for a year—but I knew within my first two weeks in Jackson that one year in Wyoming would not be enough. It has now been a decade.

During my first few years in Wyoming, I'm ashamed to admit that I rarely left Jackson Hole, so agog was I over the mountains outside my front door and remembering from the drive out how barren much of the rest of the state seemed (at least the areas around I–80). But then my brother moved to Colorado Springs, and, if I wanted to visit him, driving—via I–80—was the easiest way. While seeing Rob was great, it wasn't actually the best part of the trip. Surprisingly, the "best part" honor went to that seemingly barren land along I–80. It didn't seem as desolate as it had on the initial drive out. In fact, this time I thought it was downright beautiful. It was beautiful to look for miles in any direction and see nary a fence. It was beautiful to stop my car—no longer an oil-guzzling Jeep Cherokee—on a narrow strip of a road, cut the engine, and experience deafening silence. It was beautiful to meet a stuffed emperor penguin that had served as a hotel's mascot for more than fifty years. It was beautiful to appreciate that this land hadn't changed much since pioneers on the Oregon, Mormon, and California Trails passed through in the nineteenth century.

Giddy with newfound love for the previously neglected parts of my adopted state, I went rather crazy exploring. In the process I found the sort of small stuff that travel articles and tourism brochures overlook in favor of Wyoming biggies like Old Faithful, the mountains, the Cody Shootout, and Devil's Tower. I discovered curiosities such as a split-personality lake that drains into both the Atlantic and Pacific Oceans, sand dunes that sing, and mud believed to heal everything from skin cancer to acne. I learned that, even though Wyoming's 500,000 residents (for comparison that's less than half the population of the Denver area) are outnumbered 5:1 by their state's acreage, they don't let that stand in the way of their being every bit as offbeat as their land. For every underground ice pit or disappearing river, there's a Wyomingite who discovered the jackalope, can't stop counting, built a house entirely out of formaldehyde bottles, or welcomed Jovians by establishing an intergalactic spaceport.

Of course I still love the mountains outside my front door—they are a constant welcome distraction, even as I attempt to finish up this introduction—but I've come to realize that they define Wyoming about as much as the Eiffel Tower defines Paris. The real story of the state lies in curiosities like the final resting place of a pygmy demon and the bar where the worst country-and-western band in the Western Hemisphere plays to a packed house every Sunday night. I hope you enjoy reading it.

SOUTHWEST

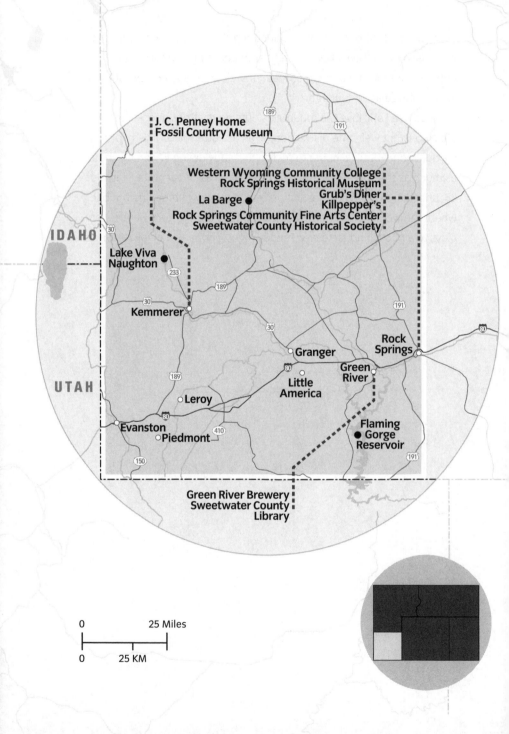

J. C. Penney Home
Fossil Country Museum

189

191

Western Wyoming Community College
Rock Springs Historical Museum
Grub's Diner
La Barge ●   Killpepper's
Rock Springs Community Fine Arts Center
Sweetwater County Historical Society

IDAHO

30

Lake Viva
Naughton ●

233

189

30   Kemmerer

30

191

80

Rock
Springs

Granger

UTAH

189

80
Little
America

Green
River

Leroy

Evanston
   Piedmont

410

Flaming
● Gorge
Reservoir

150

191

Green River Brewery
Sweetwater County
Library

0   25 Miles

0   25 KM

SOUTHWEST

I know it might be tempting to spend your entire time here staring at Rock Springs' *The Painting That Should Have Been Burned* or sipping carbonated water served up directly from Mother Nature outside Leroy, but try to pull yourself away. After all, this southwestern part of Wyoming also has ghosts, albeit rather malodorous ones, waiting to meet you (in Green River) and a two-bodied sheep looking for some love (Kemmerer). And, while Green River's invitation to Jovians to alight at its Intergalactic Spaceport hasn't yet been accepted, you never know.

Anything to Draw a Crowd
Evanston

Back when trains were the way to travel, railroad towns enticed passengers to get off and spend time with them every which way they could. There was gambling, entertainment, houses full of ladies looking for the right man (or just any man), and saloons. Evanston one-upped all the other towns, though. No, its saloons weren't necessarily better, nor were the odds of winning big in a game of blackjack. Evanston had a bear. And train passengers loved it. Travelers would pile off the train as soon as it pulled into the Evanston station to get a close-up glimpse of the bruin chained to the front of the depot . . . and if they were suitably impressed, perhaps they would stay and enjoy more of the town. Today, there's no bear chained up at the train depot, but the picturesque Bear River flows right through town and is definitely worth a stop.

Fishy Finger
Flaming Gorge Reservoir

It was a day of fishing gone really, really, really bad. In July 1991 Robert Lindsey lost his thumb, index, and middle fingers in a boating accident. The index and middle fingers were promptly recovered—all the fingers had been cut off by a boat propeller—and reattached. The thumb was presumed to be gone forever. However, six months later, just as Robert was beginning to settle into a one-thumb life, it was found . . . inside a fish. An unnamed fisherman doing some winter casting on the reservoir caught a six-pound lake trout. While preparing it for dinner, he found something unexpected in the fish's belly: Robert Lindsey's perfectly preserved, six-month-old thumb.

A process called saponification is most likely responsible for preserving the thumb. Saponification occurs only in moist, dark places (deep, cold-water lakes are perfect) and causes flesh to take on a chemical condition similar to that of soap. Sweetwater County officials guessed that the trout ate the thumb less than twenty-four hours before it was caught. The statistical likelihood of Robert's getting his thumb back in such a manner six months after the accident was about the same as winning a national lottery.

Maps Tell the Story
Granger

You don't even really have to blink to miss the tiny town of Granger today. Home to fifty-four households and 146 people as of the 2000 census, Granger was once the most important town in the state—judging by maps, at least. If you look at an early road map of the state, you'll notice that "Granger" is written in larger type than every other town and city, including the state capital, Cheyenne. Granger was indeed a hangout and/or stopover for four important nineteenth-century groups—fur trappers, pioneers, Pony Express riders, and the railroad—and both Horace Greeley and Mark Twain stopped here when passing through via stagecoach, but chances are the large type was just a misprint. Or perhaps the typesetter was a native Grangerian looking to liven up his hometown. Granger's population never reached more than a few thousand.

Today, Granger is best known for its 1856 stage station. A state historic site, the station is the exact same adobe-covered, limestone-walled structure in which Huck Finn's creator and Horace Greeley whiled away a few hours. It's at the west end of town.

A Municipal Parking Lot . . . of Sorts

Green River

It's a pretty convenient parking lot Green River has right downtown. Residents fortunate enough to rent one of the 141 spaces here can head out of town and into the hills without dealing with any traffic—not that there's ever been a recorded horse jam in history. This particular downtown "parking area" is a horse corral. As far as Green River knows, it is the only downtown city-owned horse corral in the country.

The Green River Municipal Horse Corrals, which has been around since the 1930s, used to be at the southern edge of town. But the area has grown up so much that the horses are now pretty well smack in the middle of everything. It harkens back to the days when every Wyoming town had hitching posts dotting its downtown and the only horse-power was the kind generated by animals, not V-8 engines.

It's definitely a parking lot unlike any other.

Neither the horses nor their owners seem to mind the growth, though. The corrals (each of which can hold two horses) are on the banks of the Green River, with a greenway leading right out to the foothills of the Red Desert Mountains. Kids and families are always wandering through, petting and feeding the horses, especially in spring, after foals are born.

Even though he's been a resident for twenty-odd years, Buster, the great-grandson of Roy Rogers's horse Trigger, is always a crowd-pleaser. Owned by Green River resident Bob Trujillo, Buster never reached the movie-star status his great-grandfather did, but he has had a good career as a stud. For those who want to do more than look and pet, several owners offer riding lessons right on the premises. It's not unheard of for students to start out not knowing how to ride and then to graduate to owning their own horse and having a stall of their own at the corrals.

While horses need not have a Hollywood pedigree like Buster to get into Green River's corrals, they can't just trot over here and make themselves at home. First there is the issue of the yearlong (on average) waiting list. Then there is the corral upkeep required of owners: Each 40-by-40-foot corral must be completely cleaned each week and follow uniform guidelines pertaining to siding, buildings, and colors. Each owner has to provide his or her horse with a roofed, three-sided shelter. It's enough work to make parking in the big city look easy . . . but still not as interesting. Cars don't eat sugar cubes out of your hand, and it's unlikely that a car could claim a direct relation to Trigger.

You're Not Lost
Green River

If, while driving through downtown Green River, you look up and see a building reminiscent of Chicago's famous Water Tower, don't think you took a really, really wrong turn a while back. It may be a thousand miles from the Windy City, but Green River does indeed have its own bit of Chicago in the form of a Water Tower–esque building.

Green River's version was made from locally quarried stone and was more a beer tower than a water tower. It was built in 1900 as the home of Wyoming's first brewery, the Sweetwater Brewing Company. During its peak Sweetwater Beers were popular around the country. The brewery bottled nearly 20,000 bottles a day until Prohibition put it out of business. Prohibition is now long gone, and the Green River Brewery is back; its building is now listed on the National Register of Historic Places.

Quench your thirst and grab a bite to eat here (48 West Railroad Avenue; 307–875–5255).

Neighborly Kindness
Green River

It's a good thing the good folks in Green River did it, because as far as I know, no one else in the country stepped up to help the Jovians when their planet was threatened by collisions with as many as six meteors. In 1994 the National Aeronautics and Space Administration determined that sometime between July 18 and July 24 of that year the planet Jupiter would be struck by up to six comets and/or meteors of indeterminable size. The mayor and city council of Green River, remembering back to their high-school-science days, knew that it was just such a collision with an asteroid sixty-five million years ago that is thought to have resulted in the extinction of many plant and animal species here on Earth. They surmised that the Jovians might want to jump ship before their own planet suffered such disastrous consequences. So, on July 5, 2004, by a vote of five to two, the Green River city council passed a resolution (Resolution No. R94–23) allowing any citizens of Jupiter to take sanctuary in their town.

The resolution further stipulated:

1. The Mayor, City Administrator, and appropriate staff are here authorized to contact the National Aeronautics and Space Administration (NASA), which has a budgetary account in the tens of millions of dollars dedicated to the search for intelligent life in space, and request that they broadcast this offer to the possible residents of our sister planet;
2. Since an event of this import so requires, the emergency aircraft landing field, just south of our city, be officially designated the Greater Green River Intergalactic Spaceport;
3. All residents of the City of Green River be encouraged to observe this momentous event and prepare themselves to make welcome any refugees who might cast themselves upon our mercy.

George Eckman, the then-mayor of Green River, told the Rock Springs *Rocket-Miner*, "I feel it is a gesture that could be made and should be made by someone on the planet Earth to fellow citizens of the solar system."

The two city council members who objected to the resolution did so because Green River lacked a special permit to designate a spaceport and because the arrival of Jovians would heighten an already difficult illegal-alien problem. Objectors also pointed out that experts had predicted that the meteorites threatening Jupiter would likely do very little damage to the planet and that there was already a housing shortage in the area. They were also concerned that the new residents might not be able to integrate into the local workforce.

While no Jovians sought sanctuary in Green River from the 1994 meteor strikes, the Green River Intergalactic Spaceport remains open, ready to accept any and all visitors from outer space.

Fiction Come to Life
Green River

Sweetwater County Library has ghosts outside of its fiction department. In 1993 librarians here started a "Ghost Log," detailing a series of bizarre occurrences—moans heard in a deserted ladies' bathroom, security gates inexplicably slamming shut, finicky computers and other electronics, strange odors (cigar smoke, fish, women's perfume), gusts of wind coming out of the book drop, and flickering lights. While a few of the Ghost Log reports are undoubtedly pranks, paranormal investigators have studied the library on three separate occasions. Their conclusion? There's nothing fictional about the library ghosts.

Ghosts haven't taken up residence at the library willy-nilly, though. The local hypothesis is that the spirits belong to the people buried at the old city cemetery, which was used from the 1870s to 1913 . . . and on top of which the library was built. All of the bodies as well as their attendant grave markers were ostensibly moved from here to a new cemetery in 1926. In the 1940s homes for returning World War II veterans were built on top of the vacated cemetery, and veterans and their families lived here—unhaunted—for several years. The homes were removed when they were no longer needed, and the space was vacant until library construction started in 1978. Almost immediately, construction workers unearthed twelve bodies, which were promptly reinterred at another cemetery in town.

But those weren't the last of the departed to make their way back to light. A maintenance man doing some landscaping in 1983 found some bones that turned out to be three adults and one infant. A remodeling in 1985 through 1986 uncovered a small casket with a perfectly preserved baby inside. The most recent proof that this old cemetery was perhaps moved a little too hastily came in the 1990s when construction on the street outside the library exposed the remains of a forty-ish man and woman. It kind of brings new meaning to "Build it and they will come."

The cemetery that started it all.

The ghosts seem to understand that the library and its various con-struction/maintenance activities mean them no harm or disrespect. Librarian Micki Gilmore, the current keeper of the Ghost Log, says she has never gotten the sense that the ghosts don't like the library or any people there. Out of the hundred-plus entries in the Ghost Log, the most injurious is a randomly unleashed odor of rotting fish that several staff members and patrons have reported smelling in different areas of the building at different times. And while this odor hasn't been reported in either the men's or the women's bathroom, enough door slammings, cries, and rustlings have been heard that some people would rather hold it than venture into the restroom by themselves. Drink up and then meet the ghosts yourself at 300 North First East in downtown Green River. Phone (307) 875–3615 for library hours.

The Most Important Mineral You've Never Heard Of
West of Green River

Wyoming has quite an interesting mining history spanning the periodic table—copper, silver, uranium, gold (in 1928 we even had a minor gold rush to a chicken farm outside Casper after a wheat-grain-size piece of gold was discovered inside one of its chickens in a city meat market). Today's mining activities are slightly less interesting, albeit very impor-tant to our everyday lives.

Wyoming produces nearly the entire world's supply of trona. What's trona? you might ask. Well, it's a mineral used to produce everything from glass to cleansers, detergents, pulp and paper, and aluminum, to name but a few of the everyday necessities that wouldn't be possible without Wyoming's vast trona reserves. About half of the twenty million tons of trona mined in Wyoming annually go to glassmaking. The chemical industry uses another five million tons every year. Part of the remainder of Wyoming's trona production is quite possibly in your refrigerator: Baking soda is another product that would be impossible without trona.

Wyoming's trona history started fifty million years ago, when a 15,000-square-mile lake (that's only slightly smaller than Lake Erie and Lake Ontario combined) covered much of what is today southwest Wyoming. A volcanic explosion in the Absaroka Range of the Rocky Mountains deposited thousands of feet of volcanic ash and sediment in the lake. After a gestational period of several million years, trona was born when this volcanic ash combined with excessive amounts of carbon dioxide created by decaying plant material and increased lake temperatures. The lake eventually disappeared. Its trona legacy was discovered here in 1938. The first trona mine opened in 1947.

If you're worried that extracting twenty million tons of the stuff annually sounds like too much, fear not. Wyoming is estimated to have 127 *billion* tons of trona. Even though only forty billion of these are currently considered recoverable, that still leaves the state with enough reserves to last 2,350 years. So, there's no need to worry that you're going to run out of baking soda anytime soon.

The state's trona mines are west of Green River, although you can't see much from the surface since all trona mining is done underground. The first, and still largest, mine is north of Interstate 80 at exit 72.

Not Quite the Sears Tower
About 25 miles east of Rock Springs

Don't miss a look at Wyoming's tallest building. Thankfully, it's easy to spot . . . as long as you know you're looking for a twenty-four-story-tall smokestack that is almost constantly billowing smoke and rises high above the otherwise empty desert. That's right, Wyoming's loftiest building isn't an overly ambitious capitol building or some chichi condo development with a rooftop pool, expansive views, and uniformed concierges. Ours burns coal (about five million tons a year), spews smoke, and generates power for about one million people annually.

The Jim Bridger Power Plant's smokestack has been recognized as the state's tallest building since its construction in the 1970s. But Arizona has another man-made, non-building structure that dwarfs it. Check out the Northeast chapter to see what that is.

Jim Bridger Power Plant, the state's tallest building.

BIRDS WILL MIGRATE

A black granite, marketed as Wyoming Raven, quarried from outside Wheatland was taken to Seattle and used in the construction of Bill and Melinda Gates's home.

It All Adds Up

Kemmerer

Today, you can count on one hand Wyoming's shopping malls (none of which are anywhere around Kemmerer), but back in 1902 a retail giant was born right here. In that year James Cash Penney scraped together every last nickel he had to bring his wife and son to join him in Kemmerer and help him found a dry-goods store.

He wasn't looking to start an empire, though. He was actually more concerned with morals than money. The twenty-seven-year-old Penney opened the appropriately named Golden Rule store to, well, follow the Golden Rule: Treat others as you would wish to be treated.

At the time, Kemmerer was a scattered mining community with about 1,000 residents, a company store (which operated on credit), and twenty-one saloons, which were the recipients of most residents' money. The Golden Rule store was revolutionary not only for its customer service policy but also because Penney operated on a "cash only" policy *and* offered quality merchandise at low prices, which were the same for everyone regardless of their social status. The other businessmen in the town scoffed at all of this, but especially at the cash-only idea, saying that miners and their families could never afford to shop at a store that didn't extend credit.

Those other businessmen couldn't have been more wrong. The miners and their families loved Penney's retail philosophy. His first day's sales totaled $467 . . . almost all in pennies, nickels, dimes, quarters, and half dollars. It was only $33 shy of the $500 in savings Penney had put up to open the place. That was only the beginning, though. Over the next decade new Golden Rule stores opened, and by 1912 there were thirty-four scattered across the country. In 1913 the store's name was changed to J.C. Penney Company. In 1915 sales equaled almost $5 million. By 1929 there were 1,400 J.C. Penney stores and a thriving mail-order business that sold $43 million of high-quality, low-cost merchandise annually. The J.C. Penney mother store is still open and thriving in downtown Kemmerer, and his restored house, located on Penney Avenue, is a National Historic Landmark.

A Tail of Two Bodies

Kemmerer

Ranchers in Wyoming are used to seeing some pretty strange things, whether real or imagined (the mind can go to some pretty far-off places when there's nothing but sage for miles around), but nothing could prepare rancher William Buckley for what greeted him one chilly spring morning in 1940. Checking on his flock of sheep, Buckley noticed he had two newcomers. Kind of. He had two new lamb bodies, but only one new lamb head. The two bodies shared the same head.

No, you're not experiencing double vision—this little guy has two sets of legs.

Two-bodied Lamb

Not surprisingly, the two-bodied lamb didn't live long. But, realizing he had something pretty darn unique, Buckley didn't just bury it/them in the backyard. He had the lamb(s) mounted, and today they live in the Fossil Country Museum (400 Pine Avenue; 307–877–6551). The museum also has a *Hadrosaurus* footprint, a replica coal mine, an early-1900s period dining room, and bootlegging stills—but really, how can anything compare to a two-bodied lamb?

Watch for Wildlife
North of Kemmerer

Past Lake Viva Naughton you have to watch for more than the usual numbers of wild animals. There's a corner here that is completely over-run by bears. Stuffed bears. Rumor has it that the first teddy bear was left by an elderly gent in remembrance of a small child who died there. Others evidently liked the idea and added their own bears to the alfresco collection. In recent years other species, including a unicorn and a dragon, have begun to show up as well. You can add your own animal to Teddy Bear Corner by taking Highway 233 north from Kem-merer past Lake Viva Naughton. After the road turns to dirt, drive 5 more miles—you can't miss the bears collected in a corner.

Practicing Penmanship
La Barge

It's not bad for someone who supposedly couldn't read or write. In fact, mountain man Jim Bridger's "signature" on Names Hill could teach today's doctors a few things about neat handwriting. On a soft lime-stone face with thousands of other names and signs scratched into it, illiterate Bridger's etching is perhaps the most legible and neat of all.

The "register" of the Lander Cutoff section of the Oregon Trail, Names Hill bears the marks left by pioneers as well as Native Americans and trappers traveling through this area. Thirteen thousand emigrants passed by here in 1859, the first year the Lander Cutoff was open. Not one to follow established trails, Bridger stopped by earlier, in 1844; the oldest signature dates from 1822. Names Hill is 6 miles south of La Barge on U.S. Highway 189.

16

NO TRAFFIC JAMS HERE

Kemmerer enjoys the honor of being the only town in Lincoln County with stoplights. But if you blink a little slower than usual, you could still miss both of them.

Old Time Soda Pop
Leroy

Wyoming has plenty of old-time soda fountains, but the one here in Leroy is in the running for the world's absolute oldest soda fountain. It's been around since before the railroad came here. Leroy's soda fountain was spewing before even the first European trapper set foot west of the Mississippi or Columbus sailed his three ships across the Atlantic to the New World. In fact, no one really knows when Leroy's soda fountain was established, since it is completely courtesy of Mother Nature.

When the railroad did finally make it here, Leroy was one of the passengers' favorite stops because of its fountains, where spring water bubbled up from the ground naturally carbonated. VIP passengers were allowed off here and offered a sip of the bubbly water mixed with a little lemon and sugar. You don't need to be a VIP to enjoy the soda springs today, but you do need to be willing to sleuth them out. Several are still in existence, although others have been lost due to mining. The largest one is between Piedmont and Spring Valley.

Wyoming Oasis

Little America

If every near-death experience were like S. M. Covey's, the country would be a much more civilized place, with a luxury room, 32-inch digital flat-screen television, goose-down pillows, velvet drapes, room service, and a heated outdoor pool for all. His brush with hypothermia here led directly to the founding of the town/140-room resort/über–travel center called Little America.

In the 1890s, while working this stretch of prairie as a sheepherder, Covey was caught in a blizzard. The winds were blowing at 50 miles per hour, and the temperatures were forty degrees below zero. He thought, quite rightly, that he was going to die, along with most of his flock. Not willing to freeze without a fight, Covey hunkered down for the night, all the while dreaming of a roaring fire, warm blankets, and hearty food. "How nice would it be if someone actually built some sort of shelter here?" he thought. Against the odds, he survived to see the next day and the end of the blizzard. With the whiteout conditions gone, Covey was able to find his way back to his base camp.

No one knows how much longer Covey's career as a sheepherder lasted. He lived a fairly uneventful life until the 1930s, when seeing a picture of Admiral Byrd's "Little America" in Antarctica triggered the memory of his near-death experience on the Wyoming prairie. Inspired by Byrd's polar paradise, and with more to invest than a sheepherder's salary, Covey decided that he would be the one to build the shelter he had dreamed about the night he nearly died.

In 1934 Covey's Little America—naturally named after Admiral Byrd's Antarctic venture—opened on the Wyoming plains. It had twelve rooms, two gas pumps, and a twenty-four-seat cafe. No one would be at the mercy of the weather in this spot again. Today, Little America has grown to 140 rooms as well as its own incorporated town.

The town even has a mascot, albeit not the one Covey originally had in mind. Thinking a penguin would fit well with his Antarctic–inspired idea, he arranged to have Emperor the penguin shipped to Wyoming, via Boston, from Antarctica. Unfortunately, Emperor died en route to Boston. Obviously not one to give up, Covey ordered Emperor stuffed and shipped out to Wyoming anyway. Today, the penguin stands on a block of fake ice in a sealed glass case in a hallway on the hotel's ground floor.

Of course, this stretch of prairie isn't the only place where lost and weary travelers might be looking for shelter. Little Americas have also popped up in Cheyenne, Salt Lake City, and Flagstaff. But since there's only one Emperor, those hotels are left with Emperor imitators in their lobbies.

STRIKE IT RICH

Butch Cassidy and the Hole-in-the-Wall Gang reportedly buried gold near Piedmont when pursuing lawmen were a little too close on their tail. Many have looked for it, but no one has yet found it.

A Bridge of a Different Sort
Piedmont

Railroad ties have been reclaimed to make everything from floors to fence posts, so why not reinvent retired railroad cars as well? Back when two railroad flatcars had done all they could for the Union Pacific, the good town of Piedmont found itself in need of a new bridge. It didn't take long to put two and two together: Piedmont got a new bridge, and the railroad flatcars got a new life. The two flatcars were mounted side by side—each being a lane—on concrete pillars and finished with a wood deck on top. They're still standing, 4 miles toward Piedmont from the I–80 exit. Given how well this bridge worked out, a similar one was built ½ mile north of I–80 at the same exit. Both of these bridges are getting old, though. Do you wonder what they'll be in their next life?

Sign(s) of the Times
Rock Springs

Cats and their nine lives have nothing on the sign stretching over a street in downtown Rock Springs. The banner is now enjoying its third or fourth life (whether you count three or four depends on how you measure its time spent living in a weed patch). Most likely first built and erected in the 1920s, the sign originally was an advertisement for coal, the town's most abundant and celebrated export. White letters on a red background alerted people to the town's special place in the prediesel railroad world: ROCK SPRINGS COAL, the sign read. By the 1960s coal was out of fashion, the coal mines were mostly gone, and Rock Springs was in a bit of an economic slump. The sign only seemed to remind the town of its better, coal-crammed days. It was taken down.

The sign sat in obscurity for a few years, until the Rock Springs campus of Western Wyoming Community College decided to put it to use. ROCK SPRINGS COAL was replaced by WWCC, and for years the revamped sign happily welcomed students, families, and guests to WWCC. Eventually, though, the school replaced it with a more academic-looking stone entrance, and the sign was sent to sit in the weeds at the old fairground. Seven or eight years ago, a woman walking her dog happened upon it. With the town no longer sensitive to the fact that its coal-boom days were over, historically minded citizens proud of Rock Springs' past started a drive to get the sign refurbished. The crusade was successful, and the neon ROCK SPRINGS COAL sign that now welcomes you to historic downtown was born.

Welcoming, like open arms.

And what about the entrance to Western Wyoming Community College? Mere carved stone couldn't take the place of the historic ROCK SPRINGS COAL/WWCC arch. To create the same level of visual interest, the school added a cast of the state's official dinosaur, *Triceratops,* as well. The original that this cast was made from was found in the eastern part of the state in 1889.

Losing a Namesake
Rock Springs

If you have a giant drain plug and several billion gallons of water, you might be able to help Rock Springs get its namesake back. The rock springs that the town was named after have been dry for about a century. It's not that their water ran out, but rather that their route to the surface was destroyed. That's where the giant—and we really mean giant—drain plug comes in.

While Rock Springs' springs were never a giant waterfall or such, they were still cool, clear, and wet—enough so to be a very welcome stop, and landmark, on several pioneer trails in the mid-1800s. Thousands of travelers quenched their thirst here. But there was no Environmental Protection Agency around at the turn of the last century to look out for the springs and warn that the extensive mining going on in and around Rock Springs might adversely affect them. In the early 1900s miners digging below the city reached and unknowingly destroyed the source of the springs. Thankfully, there were other sources of water around by then.

If you want to see where the springs would come out if the drain-plug idea worked, head north on Spring Drive for about ¾ mile past Dewar Drive.

Melting Pot
Rock Springs

If you're a high schooler and think today's language requirements for graduation are tough, you should have been in Rock Springs in the 1930s. While there were no fluency requirements per se, if you wanted to be able to communicate with your classmates, you'd have to know fifty-six different languages! Rock Springs was the Melting Pot of the West, and in the 1930s—when the town was its most diverse—the high school had students born in fifty-six different countries, including most European nations as well as Japan, Thailand, and China. The international students weren't exactly here on an exchange program, though; most of them came to town with parents who were working for the Union Pacific (UP) Coal Company. Rock Springs had several coal mines, including one that was the country's largest-ever mine operating through one opening. All told, the UP mines here produced about 2,000 tons of coal a day for forty years. They needed as many workers as they could get.

To celebrate the town's diversity, Rock Springs organized International Day in the 1930s. The annual celebration included a display of the different flags from all of the home countries of Rock Springs High School students. The woolen flags used in that celebration are in storage at the Sweetwater Historical Center, but less delicate ones are hanging at the Rock Springs Historical Museum (201 B Street; 307–362–3138).

While the Chinese population was Rock Springs' largest international minority, there is now no trace of the nearly 1,000 Chinese who once lived here. Other minority groups were made to feel welcome, but because of the more divisive cultural and religious differences between Westerners and the Chinese, the Chinese were persecuted; in 1885 there was even a Chinese massacre in Rock Springs that resulted in numerous deaths and the state's governor calling in help from President Grover Cleveland. After the massacre most members of the Chinese community moved elsewhere. Many of the other emigrants, though, stayed around even after the mines died off. It's not totally unheard of to walk Rock Springs' streets today and hear Japanese or Euskara (the language of the Basques) spoken, although today's speakers—fifth-generation Rock Springers by now—do so with an American accent.

Keeping It in the Family
Rock Springs

The Skorups set out to save their son from working Rock Springs' coal mines and ended up creating a Rock Springs institution . . . not to mention one of the best burgers around. The Skorups had already lost one son in Rock Springs' coal mines, and they didn't want to risk losing their sole surviving son (out of thirteen kids) the same way. But back in the 1940s, Rock Springs didn't have too many non-mine jobs for young men. The Skorups didn't want Nick, aka "Grub," to work the mines, but neither did they want him to leave the area. They did the only reasonable thing parents could do: They created a job just for Grub.

The Skorups opened a diner and gave Grub no choice but to work there by naming it Grub's Diner. The diner became much more than a job for Grub, though; he made a career out of it, serving up the diner's signature burger, the "Shamrock"—a ¼-pound beast with two patties and a side of nearly one pound of hand-cut fries—until he died in 1992. (The burgers are called Shamrocks because the place opened sometime around St. Patrick's Day; the name was supposed to be a temporary advertising gimmick, but it just kind of stuck.)

After Grub died, his widow took over. It was during her reign that the diner celebrated its fiftieth anniversary, when 3,000 or so people waited in line for hours to buy bagfuls of Shamrocks and fries. When Grub's widow died, his son and daughter-in-law, Dave and Marcy, took over. They've been at the helm for six years now. Dave, of course, grew up working at the diner. Marcy rarely fails to point out that when she and Dave first started dating, he told her she'd never work at Grub's. "Now I know that 'never' is twenty-two years," she laughs.

Grab some grub.

While prices have gone up in the sixty years since Grub's opened—a Shamrock started at 30 cents and is now $5.25—little else, including the menu and how the potatoes for fries are peeled and hand-cut every morning, has changed. Grub's is at 415 Paulson Street. Call (307) 362–6634 for information.

It's All in the Name
Rock Springs

It's never a bad idea to give your soon-to-open nightclub some local flavor, is it? Well, if you're in Rock Springs and the local feature you want to immortalize is Killpecker Creek, then yes, local flavor is a bad idea.

One of the main waterways in Rock Springs (the other being Bitter Creek), Killpecker Creek eventually empties into the mighty Green River. In the 1970s a group of nightclub owners latched onto "Killpecker's" as a great name for their club. Thinking it might be interesting to have a bit of information about this Killpecker guy who was famous enough to have had a pretty major creek, and now a club, named after him, the owners went looking for him back in history. History had no Mr. Killpecker, though. It did have plenty of documented instances in which the high levels of saltpeter in Killpecker Creek had had unfortunate effects on male "vitality." Not wanting their establishment to have the same effect on men, the club's founders immediately changed the spot's name to Killpepper's.

Stop by and see for yourself whether the name change worked: Killpepper's is at 1030 Dewar Drive. For more information phone (307) 382–8012.

Killpepper's
FINE FOOD & SPIRITS

KARAOKE TUE- WED
PITCHERS S3 5-10

R   B
E   A

The original name wasn't so fine for some would-be patrons.

WYOMING AT SEA

The U.S. Navy has had four sea vessels bearing the name Wyoming. The third *Wyoming* distinguished itself the most, participating in both World War I and World War II. In the latter war the gunnery training ship fired off more ammunition than any other ship in the fleet.

Stealing the Show
Rock Springs

Almost anywhere else, pieces by artists such as Grandma Moses, Norman Rockwell, Rufino Tamayo, Salvador Dalí, and Conrad Schwiering would be a big draw. At Rock Springs' Community Fine Arts Center, though, these paintings play second fiddle to a painting that (1) depicts local bars and prominent figures and (2) is titled *The Painting That Should Have Been Burned*. The painting was originally named *The Worldly Chapel*, but, at its second showing, an onlooker remarked that it was so bad it should have been burned the first time it was on display. Artist Darryl Newton liked this particular bit of criticism and gave his painting a second name. But the painting doesn't draw more attention than Dalí's because of its unusual name or because it is poorly painted.

The Painting That Should Have Been Burned actually isn't at all bad in its execution. In fact, it's quite good. Darryl is a talented artist whose work is found in collections across the country. What the complaining viewer, as well as some of Rock Springs' judges and law enforcement officers, found bad was the subject matter: Darryl's painting isn't merely of local bars and people, but of local bars and people during Rock Springs' "Sin City" days in the 1970s, when vice and corruption were so rampant that the town was the subject of a Wyoming grand jury investigation and a *60 Minutes* feature. Darryl painted it all for posterity . . . in a fairly accurate way. Newton admits only to incorporating

Artist Darryl Newton doesn't at all mind the controversy surrounding his painting.

four actual portraits into the piece—himself, his brother, a pool player, and one bar patron—but Rock Springers say there are some other striking resemblances that can't be the accidents that Darryl claims they are. Locals can also pick out parts of area bars in the painting.

The uproar over the painting started the moment the Community Fine Arts Center acquired it in 1978. The public outcry was so great that the painting went into hiding: It was hung in the director's office, to be viewed only by those who specifically requested to do so. In November 1985 the piece was brought out again, in the mistaken hope that the furor had died down. It was during this showing that *The Worldly Chapel* got its new name. Obviously, some people were still quite upset that the skeletons in their closets were captured in oil paint. However, despite the continued hullabaloo, the painting was kept out and remains on permanent display as part of the center's collection.

While some art collections are founded to invite controversy and outrage, this collection—despite the uproar Darryl's painting has engendered—was not. Elmer Halseth, a Rock Springs High School science teacher, started it in 1939 to give his students a project. To raise the money to buy their first painting, *Shack Alley* by Chicago artist Henrietta Wood, students had nickel-and-dime donation jars, held bake sales, and collected and sold scrap metal. New pieces were acquired whenever students had raised enough money. By 1965 their fund-raising efforts had been so fruitful that the collection was too valuable to be kept at the school any longer. The Community Fine Arts Center opened the following year to provide a more secure home for the collection, which had grown to several hundred paintings by well-known artists.

See *The Painting That Should Have Been Burned*—as well as the hundreds of others for which no one has suggested that fate—at the Community Fine Arts Center (400 C Street; 307–362–6212).

Mobile Town
Rock Springs

In a state with not even 500,000 people, a few hundred, especially when arriving in a smallish city, can make a big impact. Just ask Rock Springs. Thanks to a recent energy boom, Rock Springs has more residents than housing these days. Thankfully, it also has a quick-thinking real-estate developer and a nearly abandoned town 60 miles down I–80.

It might be in vogue to refurbish houses these days, but Rock Springs' Gerry Fedrizzi has thought of something better: *relocating* and refurbishing. With workers and families moving to Rock Springs faster than homes can be built for them, Fedrizzi realized something else had to be done. Fedrizzi noticed that Table Rock (population: 80)—a once-booming, now-busting town 60 miles west—had plenty of homes. And most of these homes just happened to be vacant. In 2005 Fedrizzi bought fifty of them from Anadarko Petroleum and quickly began moving them down the interstate to Rock Springs. By summer 2006 twenty-five of the houses had been moved, placed on new foundations, refurbished, and sold.

Unfortunately, what is good for Rock Springs is bad for Table Rock. The removal of most of its houses, even if they were unoccupied, leaves Table Rock looking even emptier than usual. In summer 2006 Table Rock's main meeting place, Table Rock Station—a combination gas station and convenience store—announced it would soon close. Know any town in need of a convenience store? We know someone who can move it.

What Used to Pass for Entertainment
Rock Springs

Hollywood, with all its glitz, glam, and stars, has nothing on Rock Springs. Brad Pitt might be easy on the eyes and Tom Hanks able to draw a laugh or a tear, but neither man, nor anyone else in Tinseltown, has been christened "The World's Greatest Entertaining Artist." Because of his skills at mimicry, magic, and ventriloquism—his dummies could talk in at least five different voices—Rock Springs' Port Jackson Ward was so named. A magic and ventriloquism show might not be as engaging today as a Brad Pitt or Tom Hanks movie—especially after you look at Ward's somewhat scary-looking dummies now living at the Sweetwater County Historical Society—but back in the early 1900s he had crowds lined up for miles to get into one of his shows.

By the age of sixteen, Ward was already one of the best magicians and ventriloquists in the world and was given the honorary title of "professor." He earned his "World's Greatest Entertaining Artist" title at age nineteen, the same year he was credited as the "Founder of Mimicry."

Today's movie stars are definitely better looking.

He was a heartthrob for early-twentieth-century European teenage girls, the Justin Timberlake of the post-Victorian age. In 1909, at the relatively ripe old age of twenty-seven, Ward held a command performance for the king and queen of England.

An emigrant to Rock Springs from England, Ward was as popular in the United States as he had been in Europe, receiving offers from Hollywood as well as booking agents across the country. But he turned it all down because Rock Springs had something better, in his eyes at least, than the glamorous life of a world-renowned entertainer: coal mining. Ward retired from traveling and performing around the world to work for the Union Pacific Coal Company. His first job with the company was loading coal. He later went on to work as a car repairman, a weighboss, and an outside foreman. Ward worked for UP for forty years, occasionally coming out of retirement to perform at local events, such as a 1916 gala celebration of the adoption of the eight-hour workday. It wasn't quite a command performance before European royalty, but evidently it was what made the World's Greatest Entertaining Artist happiest. You can find Ward's dummies at the Sweetwater County Historical Society (3 Flaming Gorge Way; 307–872–6435).

NORTHWEST

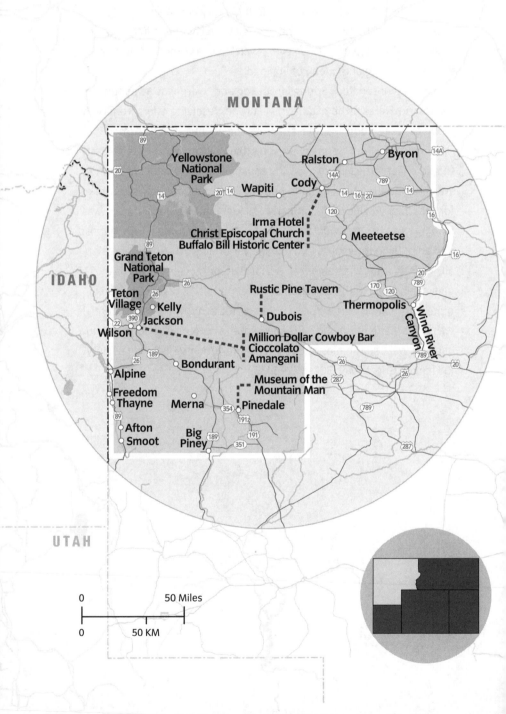

MONTANA

89

Yellowstone
National
Park

20

14

20 14 Wapiti

Ralston

14A

Byron

14A

789

Cody

14 16 20

14

120

16

Irma Hotel
Christ Episcopal Church
Buffalo Bill Historic Center

Meeteetse

16

89

IDAHO

Grand Teton
National
Park

26

20

789

Teton
Village

26

Kelly

Rustic Pine Tavern

170 120

22 390
Jackson

Dubois

Thermopolis

Wilson

Million Dollar Cowboy Bar
Cioccolato
Amangani

26

789

20

26 189

Bondurant

26

287

Wind River Canyon

26

Alpine

Museum of the
Mountain Man

Freedom
Thayne

Merna

354

Pinedale

789

89

1912

Afton
Smoot

Big
Piney

189

191

191 351

287

UTAH

0   50 Miles

0   50 KM

NORTHWEST

As a resident of one of this area's largest towns, Jackson, I like to think that the early settlers saved the best for last. More realistically, though, it was the isolated, rugged terrain and frequently harsh weather that kept homesteaders at bay for so long. Northwest Wyoming didn't see its first real residents until the eastern part of the state was setting the stage for what was to become one of the world's largest rodeos. Despite winters that brought house-burying snowstorms (which the area still gets sometimes), rocky soil unsuitable for farming, and so many mountains that it took days to get anywhere, those early pioneers—once they finally made it here—thought the area was worth the hardships.

These days, living in northwest Wyoming isn't quite the same as it was at the turn of the twentieth century. Today, residents have the benefit of nicely paved mountain passes, not to mention cars to get up and over them; space-agey synthetic fibers to keep warm and comfortable, even when the thermometer hasn't risen above zero degrees for a week; a part-time symphony orchestra; the world's largest elk-antler arch; and chichi resorts serving breakfasts that can cost up to $210. Even so, the area is still isolated—weather has closed the main airport, in Jackson Hole, for days on end; winter avalanches unexpectedly shut highways; the nearest interstate is several hours away; and sometimes it seems as though the mail comes by Pony Express. Locals wouldn't have it any other way, though. They like the isolation. Besides, any place with a birdhouse-decorated restaurant and a ski run that terrified even an astronaut is worth some time and effort to get to.

No Experience, No Problem
Afton

You'd think a plane would be a difficult thing to build without any aviation experience, but the Call brothers of Afton didn't let their shortage of sky-time deter them. Thirty-four years after the Wright brothers flew the world's first controlled airplane at Kitty Hawk, North Carolina, the Call brothers had their own aircraft airborne and were soaring over the snow-capped peaks of western Wyoming. Civil engineers and businessmen, the three brothers—Reuel, Spencer, and Barlow Call—their uncle Ivan, and friend Carl Peterson tinkered and tinkered until they had something that would stay aloft. (It took a few years and many failed attempts.)

After their successful flight, the group founded Call Aircraft Company (CallAir) in 1939 to build simple utility aircraft for farmers and ranchers. Its planes were popular workhorses until the company failed in 1962.

The CallAir Museum in Afton has several original CallAir aircraft as well as what the Call brothers turned their attention to after mastering the skies: snow cars, forerunners of snowmobiles. Unfortunately, the museum is currently in the middle of moving into a new building and won't be open to the public again until early 2008. Can't wait that long? Annually in late summer, Afton Flight Services sponsors the Star Valley Fly In, which has a show with aerobatic planes and a Young Eagles program allowing eight- to eighteen-year-olds to fly with licensed pilots for free.

Although the CallAir factory is kaput, Afton is now home to Aviat Inc., which has actually brought part of the old CallAir factory back to life and manufactures its own small leisure planes and world-class aerobatic aircraft. Aviat doesn't yet have a museum, but it does offer tours of the factory—watch the utilitarian Aviat Husky or aerobatic Aviat Pitts come together—with advance notice. Call (307) 885–3151 to make an appointment.

World's Largest Elk-Antler Arch
Afton

Don't worry, no elk were harmed in the making of this span across Afton's main street. Each winter, all male elk—which are called "bulls"—that call Wyoming home shed their antlers. Now, there are tens of thousands of elk living in Wyoming. Most of these fallen antlers are concentrated on state and federal elk feed grounds—like

World's largest elk-antler arch.

Jackson's National Elk Refuge—and are collected by the government for auction to the public. (On a side note, elk antlers are believed to be an aphrodisiac in many Asian countries, and nowadays Asian buyers dominate most of Wyoming's elk-antler auctions. On another side note, some antlers are shed in national forestlands, and the public is welcome to go "hunting" for them without the threat of arrest or hefty fines.) Before these auctions became prevalent, however, more than 3,000 antlers were given to the town of Afton to help it achieve its dream of constructing the world's largest elk-antler arch.

Arch construction began in June 1958 and was completed in July 1959. When all was said and done, there was no doubt that Afton had succeeded in its goal: Its antler arch spanned an impressive 75 feet across the entirety of Main Street and rose to a neck-craning height of 18 feet. For comparison, the four elk-antler arches marking the corners of Jackson's town square, an hour to the north, are only 10 feet wide and 13 feet tall.

Going to the Birds
Alpine

John and Francene Jensen didn't plan on their restaurant in Alpine being overrun with birdhouses; it just happened. When they bought the place eight years ago, decor was a little lacking, so Francene took the dozen or so birdhouses she had and hung them up. They were meant to be temporary, but customers liked them so much—and started donating birdhouses of their own to the collection—that before the Jensens knew it, their dozen birdhouses had multiplied to 563 birdhouses, and their restaurant became Kringle's Birdhouse Café. Included in the collection are birdhouses shaped like all fifty states, a ceramic birdhouse brought to them by regular patrons Richard and Linda Petty (yes, 200-career-NASCAR-wins Richard Petty), cowboy boot–shaped birdhouses, a basset hound birdhouse, Hawaiian coconuts turned into birdhouses, a saddle birdhouse, and even a birdhouse modeled on the exterior of the cafe.

But don't think that all these birdhouses exist only to take diners' attention away from the food. You wouldn't expect to find a master European chef serving up down-home fare in a tiny town of 600, but John Jensen started his culinary career at the Friars Club in Beverly Hills and had his own California-based catering company before landing in the Cowboy State. He fed nearly every Hollywood celebrity of the day, including Frank Sinatra, Liberace, President Gerald Ford, Dinah Shore, and Oscar-winner Frank Capra, and has taught at the Culinary Institute of America and the California Culinary Academy. While his fettuccine Alfredo is to die for, make sure to save room for dessert; a long list of customer testimonials call John's carrot and chocolate cakes nothing less than the world's best.

The Kringle's Birdhouse Café is open from 7:00 A.M. to 2:00 P.M. Monday through Wednesday, and from 7:00 A.M. to 8:00 P.M. Thursday through Sunday. It is on the south end of Alpine at 161 U.S. Highway 89. Phone (307) 654–7536 for more information.

CHOWING DOWN, CHAMPION—STYLE

Rulon Gardner, a 2000 Olympic gold medallist (and 2004 Olympic bronze medallist) in Greco-Roman wrestling, may live in Colorado Springs, Colorado, these days, but his family remains right where he grew up, in Wyoming's Star Valley. You can meet some of them at Gardner's County Village and Rulon's Burger Barn, owned by one of Rulon's brothers, and compete for a spot on "Rulon's Wall of Fame." No, you won't have to wrestle the big guy (he's 6 feet 2 inches tall and weighs 225 pounds), but you will have to eat a one-and-a-half-pound hamburger with all the trimmings, a family-size order of fries, and a large soda . . . in twenty minutes. Those who have done this are a pretty exclusive group: Rulon himself and about thirty others. Rulon's Wall of Fame includes the mugs of these champion eaters. Just south of the Burger Barn is the farm where Rulon grew up.

Rulon Gardner's wall of fame for champions—champion eaters, that is.

Icebox of the Nation
Big Piney

It's a distinction I wouldn't necessarily want my town to have: coldest year-round average temperature of any place in the United States. But the 454 people living in Big Piney don't seem to mind. The distinction did earn them—back in 1930—an official weather station belonging to the Federal Weather Bureau that is still in operation today. We don't know if global warming has been heating up Big Piney, but its average annual temperature the past few years has been around thirty degrees Fahrenheit. January is always coldest, with a monthly average temperature well below zero (!), and August is warmest, averaging a still-cool sixty degrees Fahrenheit.

A SECOND ICEBOX

Yellowstone, about 100 miles north of Big Piney, has below-freezing temperatures throughout the year. There are the usual six months of winter (starting in October) when you can reliably expect 100 percent of the days to be below freezing. However, Yellowstone still averages nineteen days below freezing in May—when most of the rest of the country is enjoying spring—and six freezing days in June. July, the warmest month, generally has two days with below-freezing temperatures; August has four freezing days; and September has fourteen.

Bring In Your Dead
Bondurant

No, you haven't had too much to drink. That indeed is a bear sitting—or, rather, slumped—in a stool up against the bar. And yes, it's dead. Not even Bondurant locals can remember exactly when this odd tradition—of hunters bringing in the black bears they've just shot for a last drink at the Elkhorn Bar—started, but it's been going on for at least forty years. And the Elkhorn Bar certainly didn't ask for this tradition to start; it just did. Over the years, the Elkhorn has hosted as many as three black bears at once . . . and dozens of unknowing, shocked patrons. Bar workers say they usually see six bears a season. Hunters celebrate their kill with whatever drink strikes their fancy.

Want to keep your distance from the bears? Stay away from the three bar stools closest to the front door. (Black bears weigh several hundred pounds, and hunters don't want to carry them any farther than necessary.) Want to *really* keep your distance? Stay away for the entirety of the black-bear-hunting season, May 1 through June 15. The Elkhorn is on Highway 191, just as you enter Bondurant from the north. Phone (307) 733–8358 for more information.

Unfaithful
Bridger–Teton National Forest, outside of Afton

Old Faithful, the eponymous Yellowstone geyser that spurts super-heated water 180 feet into the air every eighty or so minutes, might be Wyoming's most famous geyser (at least it's famous as far as geysers go, with an estimated 25 percent of all Americans visiting the area sometime during their lives and nearly three million people seeing it every year), but it is not the state's most unique geyser. Periodic Spring, outside of Afton, is North America's only cold-water geyser and is the largest of the three known fluctuation springs in the world. At full flow, 285 gallons of water per second come tumbling out. For comparison's sake, there are around 1,000 warm-water geysers, including Old Faithful, in the world (half of which are in Yellowstone).

During the fall and winter, Periodic Spring lives up to its name by turning on and shutting off every twelve to twenty minutes. Like schoolkids, though, the spring seems to take the summer off; the flows are hardly noticeable during the high-water months of May, June, July, and August. (These months are "high water" because rivers and streams are swollen with melted snow.) Despite its sporadic nature, the spring is Afton's main water supply.

As most scientists in the region are more concerned with earthquakes —the Teton Fault to the north is capable of generating a magnitude-7.5 quake—and the overdue eruption of the supervolcano that lies under Yellowstone (and is responsible for that park's warm-water geysers), no one really knows for sure what makes Periodic Spring periodic. One theory is that underground streams carry melting snow to a lake deep in the surrounding mountains of the Salt River Range. When this lake fills up enough, a natural siphon sucks the water to the surface, where it erupts out as Periodic Spring. When enough water has been drained, the siphon fills with air and the flow stops . . . until twelve to twenty minutes later, when the lake has again been topped up by more water from the underground streams.

Periodic Spring is 5 miles east of Afton, at the end of Swift Creek Road. (It's a short hike after parking at the road's terminus.)

DAM IT AND THEY WILL COME

The Buffalo Bill Dam, once the highest dam in the world, wasn't built with windsurfing in mind—crop irrigation and supplying power and water to nearby towns were actually more important to the engineers designing it—but even so, it is still one of the top-ten places to windsurf in the country. At least according to *Outside* magazine. Wind from three mountain gorges meet at the Buffalo Bill Reservoir, creating constant gales and waves. The dam is on U.S. Highways 14/16/20, just to the west of Cody.

Meant for irrigation, but a favorite spot for windsurfers too.

Home on the Range . . . or in the Forest

Bridger–Teton/Shoshone National Forest

Kayla Michael could live year-round in a house in a city, but she prefers not to. Not even the largest, most perfectly situated mansion would be as roomy or have the views of her preferred residence: outside. Backpacking in the Thorofare region of southern Yellowstone and the mountains of the Absaroka Range since 1982, Kayla says her home is the wilderness. She spends around six months out under the stars every year.

As soon as most of the snow melts, she hikes into the Thorofare region by herself, carrying a seventy-five-pound backpack. She usually brings along enough food—mac and cheese, ramen noodles, nuts, powdered milk, instant oatmeal, beef jerky—and supplies to last her a month at a time. Kayla usually comes out just two or three times, and only then to resupply, before the snow shuts her down for the year sometime in October.

Wandering around her adopted natural neighborhood—she estimates that she hikes about 1,000 miles per year—Kayla often goes for days at a time without seeing another human. She never gets lonely, though; there are plenty of animals. During the summers of 2005 and 2006, Kayla saw forty-two bears, thirty-one of which were grizzlies. While she has had some close encounters, she has never had any bad bear experiences. "I think that the grizzly is just as much afraid and wanting to avoid us as we are them," she says. She has also stumbled upon the den of one of the area's wolf packs and watched as six adult wolves took down a cow elk. While the wolves might feast, Kayla herself dines pretty simply in the backcountry; she doesn't carry a stove, preferring to make a fire if anything needs heating. After twenty-five years in the area, she's also intimately familiar with the edible plants.

Kayla's life when out of the Thorofare is also quite simple. She doesn't own a home or a car. She has a mountain bike, but it rarely comes out of storage. Kayla walks everywhere she needs to go, only occasionally taking public transportation. She lives in a rented room or a hotel. She has no cell phone. "I live in poverty, but it is by choice," she says. "I wouldn't have it any other way. The Thorofare and Absaroka mountain country is my home; you don't need money in the backcountry."

If you want to see for yourself how special the Thorofare is, spend a few days hiking on Trail No. 3053. Turn onto Buffalo Valley Road from Highway 26/287 a few miles north of the Moran entrance to Grand Teton National Park. Buffalo Valley Road dead-ends at the trailhead.

Not Quite like Parting the Red Sea, but Close
Byron

In the 1890s industrious Mormon pioneers were hard at work on the 37-mile Sidon Irrigation Canal when they ran into a problem. A big problem. In the form of a giant sandstone boulder sitting right in the middle of their prospective canalway. They had already excavated, with the help of horse-drawn plows and slip scrapers, and constructed miles of canal, and they couldn't afford to stop because, without the canal, there was no way to irrigate the thousands of acres of land they had earmarked for crop planting. According to legend, canal workers and pioneering homesteaders prayed and prayed and prayed about the rock until divine intervention caused it to split. Post-miracle, workers picked up right where they had left off, and the Sidon Canal was finished in less than two years. The split rock became known as Prayer Rock, and the canal is still in use today, carrying water from the Shoshone River to nearly 20,000 acres of farmland.

ETERNAL FLAME

In 1901 a farmer in Byron saw gas escaping from a hole dug for a fence post on his property. What he hoped to achieve by lighting the leaking gas, no one knows, but he ended up creating a minor tourist attraction. After he lit it, the hole continued to burn for several years.

Lonely Heart
Cody

Some fifty million years ago, Heart Mountain wasn't the solitary peak it is today, perched alone north of Cody. It was fully a part of the Absaroka Range, dozens of miles away. For years no one understood how Heart Mountain got to its present home. There was no doubt, however, that it had moved: Rock at the 8,123-foot peak's summit is 250 million years older than the rock at its base. Obviously, the two pieces hadn't always been joined.

Locals have plenty of theories—mostly involving aliens—but the one geologists have come up with recently makes the alien theories sound pretty plausible. Computer models show that it really could have happened, though.

Fifty million years ago, a series of volcanic eruptions in the Absaroka Range (these volcanoes are now extinct) rocked the area. Lava from these eruptions was trapped beneath a rock mass roughly the size of the Hawaiian island of Kauai, and, with nowhere to escape to, the Kauai-size chunk was eventually tilted two degrees from west to east. At the same time the rock was tilting, water-filled dikes within it—and if you haven't already guessed it, this chunk is what is now known as Heart Mountain—were also filled with lava, and the lava heated both the water and surrounding rock. The superhot water had nowhere to escape to, and the mountain began to work like a pressure cooker: As the water got hotter and hotter, the pressure continued to rise. Eventually, with nowhere to go but up, the pressure lifted the rock, and the mountain began to slide. And slide, and slide.

By the time all was said and done, Heart Mountain had left all of its neighbors 62 miles behind. And if this isn't crazy enough, Heart Mountain made this trek east in less than thirty minutes, giving it an average speed of more than 120 miles per hour. Heart Mountain is 9 miles north of Cody and is best seen from U.S. Highway Alt. 14 or from Highway 120.

The Sweetest Hotel That Ever Was
Cody

Buffalo Bill Cody was famous for killing an average of eight bison a day (for an estimated lifetime total of more than 4,000 in just seventeen months), hard riding as part of the Pony Express, battling and scalping Native Americans, and sharpshooting. It's hard to imagine a man like that having a sentimental side, but Buffalo Bill Cody did. That sentimental side lives on today at the Irma Hotel, which he named for his daughter Irma and once called "just the sweetest hotel that ever was."

Evidently Cody wasn't the only person who thought this. England's Queen Victoria thought so much of the place that she gifted it with a cherrywood bar that, even today, is one of the most photographed things in the entire town of Cody. While the Irma Hotel definitely hosted its share of the rich and famous and of European royalty (all in the area for sightseeing or hunting trips), it was also the site of auditions for Buffalo Bill's Wild West Show. While the hoity-toity were inside the hotel sipping tea and brandy, coarse cowboys were showing off their horsemanship skills and their aim—sometimes on the buffalo that could run amok in downtown Cody—on an adjacent empty lot. You can visit the most photographed bar in the state at 1192 Sheridan Avenue, although you no longer have to worry about cowboys staging target practice next door or bison running loose through downtown. For more information phone (307) 587–4221.

A bar fit for a queen.

Gambling for God
Cody

The year was 1898, and Cody's population was 190—about 20 God-fearing women and 170 godless men. With the men preferring saloons to churches, it's not surprising there were few houses of worship. In fact, there weren't any houses of worship. The improvement-minded women started campaigning to change this. Nagging their husbands—and that's the exact word the historical records use, "nagging"—the women started to get the word out that they wanted a church.

The women did such a good job of nagging—umm, persuading—that one evening at downtown Cody's Purcell Saloon, when the usual poker game had an unusually large pot, the players actually thought to stipulate that the winner donate the money to building the church of his choice. Whether this was an act of godliness or merely a way to silence the townswomen has been lost to history, but, either way, the pot provided the majority of funds with which Cody's Episcopal church was built.

Completed in 1902 the church no longer requires gambling proceeds for upkeep. In fact, in 1965 Cody's Episcopalians were able to build a larger church without needing even a few cents of poker proceeds. The poker church, a tiny white building, is no longer used for daily services but does host a number of weddings and baptisms, as well as services from June until September. Christ Episcopal Church is at 825 Simpson Avenue; call (307) 587–3849 for more information.

The church built with a poker pot.

Fields of Fact
Cody

A fast running back could sprint the length of the Buffalo Bill Historical Center (BBHC) in around a minute . . . but then he'd be missing such exhibits as a lock of Buffalo Bill's hair, actual footage from Buffalo Bill's Wild West Show, and all of the 6,500 firearms in the museum's collection.

Thousands of motorists heading to Yellowstone saw Bear 104 alive; more people see her now, though.

Cody may be a small town of 8,800, but it is home to what novelist James Michener called "the Smithsonian of the West." Within its seven acres—the equivalent of five football fields—the BBHC has more than 35,000 artifacts, 20,000 books, 260,000 photographs, 1,000 paintings, 485 sculptures, and a partridge in a pear tree. Just kidding on that last one. But the BBHC does have one stuffed grizzly: Bear 104, who was a regular alongside the highway between Cody and Yellowstone before being hit and killed by a truck.

When Buffalo Bill's niece, Mary Jester Allen, first opened the museum in a 50-foot-by-70-foot log cabin in 1927, she didn't have any idea that it would one day grow to be the centerpiece of the town named after her famous uncle. Within a few years, though, the Buffalo Bill Museum was teeming with Buffalo Bill and western-themed treasures. A second museum, the Whitney Gallery of Western Art, was added—in another building—in 1959. The original Buffalo Bill Museum moved into bigger digs in 1969. In 1979 a third museum, the Plains Indian Museum, opened, followed in 1991 by the Cody Firearms Museum, which has everything from sixteenth-century dueling pistols to guns used in television shows like *Bonanza* and *Palladin*. In 2002 the Draper Museum of Natural History, the home of Bear 104, was added to the center. Clint Eastwood came to town for the opening. But everything—even the rare Remington paintings and Annie Oakley's favorite outfit (you won't believe how small she was!)—pales when displayed next to a lock of the hair of the great buffalo hunter himself. The Buffalo Bill Historical Center is located at 720 Sheridan Avenue. For hours and other information phone (307) 587–4771.

Wooden Wonderland
Dubois

Used to be that every town in Wyoming had a real, honest-to-goodness western bar, complete with knobbled pine, leather-backed booths, more stuffed animal heads than you could count, and real cowboys—you can tell by their bowed legs—propped up against a wooden bar. They're few and far between these days, however—the western bars, not the cowboys. There's the Million Dollar Cowboy in Jackson, The Mint in Sheridan, and Dubois's Rustic Pine Tavern.

The pine-covered Rustic Pine Tavern.

The posts to tie up your horse out front are gone, but everything else is pretty much exactly as it was when the Rustic Pine Tavern was built in the 1930s. The interior—and exterior—woodwork was all done by local craftsmen, whose progeny still occasionally pop their hatted heads in. While the interior burlwood is one-of-a-kind, you'll find yourself more fascinated by the exterior wood planking. Bar owner Buck Butkovich didn't know how many split pine poles were used to cover the entire outside of the bar (it's clapboard siding underneath), so I tried to count myself. When I say "entire outside of the bar," I'm not exaggerating in the least. I stopped at 573 pine pieces (give or take 50—pieces of pine look remarkably similar) . . . and had only gotten about halfway through counting. Even the bar's name is written in pieces of pine. Mosey on over to the Rustic Pine Tavern at 119 East Ramshorn. For more information call (307) 455–2430.

It's a Zoo
Dubois

Why bother with the unpredictable wildlife hidden deep inside nearby Yellowstone and Grand Teton National Parks when Dubois has a black bear, trout, jackalope, moose, buffalo, deer, and elk . . . all no more than a few feet from a parking lot and ready to photograph? (We swear that if you take your photos from the right angle, some people won't be able to tell that these animals are plastic, fiberglass, and, in one case, stuffed.)

The Dubois Chamber of Commerce thinks Mr. Moose was the first to move into town. Taking up residence near the Laundromat on East Ramshorn, the moose was an instant hit, with its giant paddles, goofy grin, and regal bearing. Over the next two decades, as word got out among the plastic animal population about Dubois's fauna friendliness, others moved in. Drawn to the flies, a trout showed up at Whiskey Mountain Tackle. Perhaps sensing the appropriateness of the locale, a black bear moved into the parking lot of the Black Bear Country Inn. An elk began hanging out with campers at the KOA.

Tired of constantly being surrounded by dirty laundry, Mr. Moose eventually relinquished his Laundromat lookout duty to a buffalo and moved himself to a quieter location east of town. A few deer have found their ideal home on C Street, and two jackalopes, including one from the extremely rare subspecies *brightus pinkae Jackalopus,* guard the Country Store Exxon. Now there's an animal you could never photograph, or even find, in Yellowstone, no matter how hard you searched or how far you hiked.

Author Dina Mishev taking one of Dubois's animals for a ride.

Fur Folly

Fort Bonneville

In May 1832 Captain Bonneville set out from Nebraska's Fort Kearney to get into the Wyoming fur business. Arriving at the Green River with his 110 men and about twenty wagons, Bonneville grew concerned about the proximity of hostile Blackfeet and ordered his men to construct a fortified, winter-ready camp on the banks of the river. (On a side note, this group was the first to take wagons over the Continental Divide; their route through the mountains eventually became part of the Oregon Trail.) The fort was finished by early August but was abandoned before the men had time to settle in. An early snowstorm that nearly buried them showed the location to be a poor one. Bonneville and his men left, heading south.

Seasoned mountain men in the area named this disastrous endeavor "Fort Nonsense" because they believed Bonneville to be completely inept, not only at choosing a location for a fort but also at fur trading. After leaving his hastily constructed headquarters on the Green River, Bonneville and his men, novices at both trapping and dealing with Indians, were facing near starvation. Most of his men deserted, but Bonneville continued wandering a few years more. He eventually returned to his post at Fort Kearney, where he found he had been declared AWOL, absent without leave. Not wanting his military career to be over quite yet, Bonneville spent several years trying to get reinstated. Eventually, an act of Congress did the job just in time for him to join the American invasion force that captured Mexico City in 1847. But controversy followed him even there. He was court-martialed and found guilty of three of ten charges, although he received only nominal punishment. When he returned to the United States, Bonneville was sent back to Fort Kearney as commanding officer.

One would think these adventures were the biggest of Bonneville's life, but it turns out that he had saved the best for last. At age seventy-five he took a twenty-two-year-old bride. They lived happily ever after for seven more years. Bonneville ended up living about as long as the last vestiges of his foolish fort. Nothing is left anymore today, but some ruins still remained in the 1880s.

Gimme Freedom
Freedom

Polygamy is frowned upon and prosecuted by law everywhere in the United States these days, but back in 1879 when Freedom (the first settlement in Star Valley) was established, it wasn't. The Wyoming Territory had other things—Indian wars, an incredibly sparse population—to worry about.

Neighboring Idaho, however, was not so lax. Literally on the Wyoming/Idaho border, Freedom got its name from the freedom it gave Mormon polygamists living in Idaho to outrun the law. All they had to do was walk across the street and they'd be in another jurisdiction, where the nearest law enforcement officer could have been several days' ride away.

FREEDOM FACTORY

Freedom Arms, in Freedom, is Wyoming's only maker of handcrafted handguns. Crafting fewer guns in a year than the big guys do in a day, Freedom Arms is best known for its Model 83. Insurance prohibits visitors from entering the factory itself, but there's a front room with gun models and game mounts on exhibit.

Crazy Skiing
Grand Teton National Park

To those not accustomed to mountains, the Grand Teton looks barely climbable, much less skiable. In 1968 Bill Briggs, a ski instructor with a fused hip who had moved to Jackson from the East Coast, looked at the 13,770-foot mountain and wanted to ski it. Everyone thought he was crazy, and not just because of his hip. I mean, really; just look at the mountain. After Bill became the first person to actually do it, on June 16, 1971, people thought he was even crazier. Today, though, he's recognized as the father of ski mountaineering, and his ski descent route on the Grand Teton is considered a classic. Several dozen expert skiers each year now repeat his feat.

The director of the Great American Ski School at Jackson's Snow King Resort, a position he has held since 1967, Bill doesn't look the part of a ski pioneer. When he's off the slopes, you notice his limp, the result of an operation at age twenty-nine to fuse his hip. Once he's on skis, though, there's no indication of it. The rumor around Jackson is that Bill asked the doctor performing the surgery to fuse the hip in a skiing rather than a walking position. Unfortunately, it's not totally true. Bill says he did tell the doctor he wanted to continue skiing after the surgery, and the doctor, a skier himself, appreciated that. The hip was set halfway between a sitting and a standing position . . . which happened to be perfect for skiing.

Although one would think that skiing down the Grand Teton was the hardest part, Bill says it was getting up the mountain that was worst. He had already stood on the mountain's summit a good one hundred times before skiing it, "but no matter how many times you do it, going up is always the worst part," he says. Bill hadn't planned on skiing solo—he headed up with three friends—but as the group got higher and higher up the mountain, into more and more dangerous territory, everyone but Bill backed off. Several spots on the ski down are very exposed, and, if you were to fall, it would mean certain death. Bill did fall, three times, on the way down, but luckily none of his falls were in these exposed areas.

Back in town, few people believed Bill. The publisher of the local newspaper needed proof, so she flew over the mountain with Bill in an airplane. Bill's ski tracks from the summit were still visible. She took a photo that is now as famous as Bill himself.

Long retired from ski mountaineering, Bill still teaches clinics and the occasional lesson at the Snow King Ski School. You can also catch him at his other job—playing in a band—every Sunday night at the Stagecoach Bar in Wilson.

THIS TREE GOT BACK

About a mile up the hiking trail to Lupine Meadows—the trail that all people climbing the Grand Teton as well as regular day hikers ascend—is a very, very shapely tree. It doesn't even take a close look for passersby to notice that its form gives even the fittest female bodies in Hollywood a run for their money.

Not even J. Lo is this shapely.

A Mountain by Any Other Name . . .

Grand Teton National Park

In English, "Teton" sounds pretty, poetic even. The French fur trappers and explorers who named this mountain range weren't thinking pretty and poetic, though. *Téton* means "breast" in French. Obviously, when the Frenchmen stumbled upon these fair mountains, it had been quite some time since they had seen a woman and her tétons. In the 1870s a group of modest American geologists who knew their French attempted to rename the Grand Teton, the highest peak in this range, "Mount Hayden" after their expedition director. However, the new name never stuck, and, since fewer and fewer Americans know any French, most visitors to the park today have no idea they just paid an entrance fee to visit the "big boob."

The Teton Range, named by French trappers who hadn't seen a woman in a while.

Unlike most boobs, and most mountain ranges, the Tetons continue to grow. A fault running along the base of the range sends the mountains a few millimeters up and the valley a few millimeters down every year.

To be fair to the trappers who tagged these mountains as the Tetons, the range does look slightly more *téton*-esque from the west, and that was the direction from which the Frenchmen first saw them. The view from the top of the Grand Targhee Ski and Summer Resort, in Alta, Wyoming, is one of the best of the range, just in case you're looking to see if the mountains really do resemble *tétons*.

SPEAKING OF THE TETONS

For thirty years one of the mountains at Grand Targhee Ski and Summer Resort was named Mary's Nipple. The Forest Service never officially acknowledged this name, but it was official enough to be on the resort's signs. The name originated one night three decades ago when a waitress—named Mary, of course—working at the resort's Trap Bar streaked through the resort's base area. In 2003 Mary and her infamous nipple were long gone, and visitors to the resort complained about the explicitness of the mountain's name. It is now called just Mary's. Locals didn't take the name change lightly, though. A "Save Mary's Nipple" campaign was launched, and you can still see bumper stickers bearing that slogan around Jackson Hole and Alta.

Keeping Things Clean
Jackson

Leave it to the first all-female town government in the country to clean things up. Like most western towns in the early 1900s, Jackson was often mired in mud . . . and worse. Remember that the horsepower still most often in use, even as late as the 1920s, was of the natural and not the mechanical variety. The town councilors and the mayor (Mayor Grace Miller, if you want to impress friends at a cocktail party; Miller was also responsible for the initial platting of Jackson in 1901) weren't elected on an anti-muck platform, but the wooden sidewalks they built in 1920 around the town square, which itself was built in 1917, were much appreciated. The mud and dirt have long been under control, and cars have replaced horses, so today's visitors to Jackson appreciate the wooden walks more for aesthetics than anything.

Wooden sidewalks do more than look cool.

Eternal Cowboy

Jackson

Lots of people meet at the Million Dollar Cowboy Bar, right on the town square in Jackson, and hold it close to their hearts, but one bar relationship is truly unique. Robert Irvin "Bob" Whitaker's wife joins her husband there once a year. She has a bartender get Bob's ashes from the upstairs office, where some of them have been kept in a black-labeled Jack Daniels bourbon bottle since Whitaker died in 1991.

A banker from Kansas, Whitaker loved the Cowboy Bar and its kitschy western decor—a bar inlaid with 592 or 624 silver dollars (depending on who is telling the story), saddles in lieu of bar stools, numerous game mounts, and an abundance of knobbled pine—and he could think of no better place to spend eternity. Take a swirl on the dance floor in his honor. The bar is under the biggest neon lights on the town square, at 25 North Cache. For hours and other information phone (307) 733–2207.

The much-loved, even in death, Million Dollar Cowboy Bar.

MAGIC WATERS

During World War II it was thought the Germans might try to poison the water in Wyoming's Wind Rivers Mountains. To prevent such a catastrophe—this area is home to two-thirds of the country's headwaters (the Columbia, Mississippi, and Colorado Rivers)—U.S. bombers patrolled the area. The Germans never showed, and one U.S. bomber crashed.

Culinary Olympian

Jackson

You'd expect to find some Olympians—at least of the winter variety—in Jackson Hole. After all, the valley is home to one of the most challenging ski resorts in the country and is covered by snow for six months of the year. Resident Tommy Moe won gold (downhill skiing) and silver (Super G) in 1994. In 2006 twenty-year-old Resi Stiegler, daughter of 1964 slalom gold medallist and Jackson Hole resident Pepi Stiegler, competed in her first Olympics. Hans and Nancy Johnstone, now owners of the Alpine House Bed and Breakfast, competed in Nordic combined and the biathlon, respectively, in the Olympics. However, one Olympian—of a very different sort—stands out above all the others. Thirty-two-year-old Oscar Ortega won a gold medal at the 2004 Olympic Culinary Games for excellence in pastry. Yes, you read that correctly: Culinary Olympics.

Oscar competes in contests of cooking, encounters of edibles, and skirmishes of sweetness. In addition to his Olympic success, Ortega has also perfected pastries at the Restaurant of the Nations competition (where he won a silver medal), the 2006 International Pastry Masterpiece (winning a silver for his chocolate showpiece and a bronze overall), and the 2006 World Pastry Championships.

Jackson's other Olympians, the ones who throw themselves down the side of a mountain with skis strapped to their feet, don't have anything on Oscar in terms of training. He spends hours a day and often well into the night preparing for these international pastry competitions; in summer 2006 Oscar was already looking toward competitions in 2008. All of the practice pays off. Even though Oscar is frequently the youngest competitor, he now rarely finishes without winning a medal.

Some of his chocolate and sugar sculptures weigh upwards of forty pounds, and competition days are usually seventeen hours of nonstop melting, baking, lifting, and assembling. "Like any other competition, it is the training that is most intense," Oscar says. "If you haven't trained and prepared in advance, you're not going to do well." Thankfully, after three years as the pastry chef at various restaurants and upscale dude ranches in Jackson Hole (his hazelnut dark-chocolate mousse and espresso mascarpone cheesecake often made dudes forget they were in Wyoming to learn how to be rough-and-ready cowboys), Oscar opened his own pastry and chocolate shop, Cioccolato (225 North Cache; 307–734–6400), in downtown Jackson. Now he has almost all the time in the world to practice. We say "almost" only because his chocolate sculptures are such that eating one would be like taking a bite out of the *Mona Lisa*. Since no one in his or her right mind wants to do that, Oscar must make regular pastries like tiramisù, lemon tarts, raspberry mousse, and crème brulée for those who actually want to eat rather than just stare.

Shootout at the Camera Corral
Jackson

It's a pretty enviable safety record. Over the course of the Jackson Hole Shootout Gang's fifty-year and 20,000-bullet history—which makes it the longest-running shootout in the country—no one has yet been shot with a real bullet. Of course, the gang's actors play at dying several times each night. Then there was the time an actor came close to being actually hanged (a harness that was supposed to prevent a real lynching malfunctioned, and the actor was gray and gasping for air by the time fellow gang members cut him down).

The Shootout was started in 1956 as a way to draw visitors to downtown Jackson so they'd spend some time browsing, and buying, in stores, and it may be one of the most well-known and popular tourist activities in Jackson. The show certainly inspires some laughs, but the behind-the-scenes antics are even better. For example, in the early years one of the bad guys would actually do an ad-libbed detour, on horseback, through a town square toy store. While galloping through, he'd liberate a few items and then—perhaps to show that bad guys can occasionally be good—pass them out to kids watching the show.

The biggest backstage ruckus came in 1962. A true tale from that summer's season involves two of the gang's posse members riding over to DD Camera Corral during the show and attempting to rob the store for real. Luckily, real Undersheriff Bud Roice had been tipped off by an informant. Undersheriff Bud was at the Camera Corral waiting for the two fake outlaws/real attempted robbers and, when they appeared, fired a real warning shot into the air. Needless to say, the two wannabe criminals weren't expecting to be confronted by real law enforcement and real bullets. They abandoned their plan faster than you can say, "real jail."

The Shootout Gang performs on the town square at 6:15 P.M. daily (except Sunday) from Memorial Day through Labor Day. Things have gotten tamer over the years, so don't worry that you'll bear witness to any attempted real robberies.

ROBBING THE BANK FOR BREAKFAST

Jackson is known throughout Wyoming as a hoity-toity kind of place where the rich and famous play. Looking over the breakfast menu at one of the area's swankiest hotels, Amangani, does nothing to refute this. There are the $15 huckleberry pancakes, $16 eggs, and $18 huevos rancheros. Then it starts getting really crazy. The frittata is $210! (To be fair, you can get a frittata without the one-ounce dollop of sevruga caviar and sour cream for a mere $38.) You could get some decent cowboy boots for less!

Law, Wyoming Style
Jackson Hole

Gerry Spence might have once been infamous for being the first vale-dictorian of the University of Wyoming Law School to fail the bar exam. These days he's just plain famous . . . for both his fringed fashions and his lawyering. He hasn't lost a criminal case as a prosecutor or defense attorney, has obtained acquittals for former Philippine First Lady Imelda Marcos and accused white-supremacist Randy Weaver, successfully sued Kerr-McGee in the Silkwood case (arguably the case that set Gerry's star rocketing toward national fame, or at least notoriety), and once obtained a $52 million judgment against McDonald's.

Before his successes in law, and before the suede buckskin-fringed jackets (of which he has fourteen, all designed and made for him by wife Imaging, failing the bar exam wasn't the first indication Gerry had that the law might not be the thing for him. While growing up in Laramie, Gerry didn't know a single lawyer, nor did he really know what lawyers did. About all he knew was that the law gave you a lot of power; as a rebellious teen who often felt powerless, he liked the idea of shifting the balance of power. Gerry's alternate career choices weren't all that intriguing either. His mother wanted him to be a preacher, but "I loved sin too much," Gerry says. Teaching was out because he knew the trouble he had caused for his own teachers and didn't want to have to deal with similar antics from students. Nor could he follow in his father's footsteps and become a scientist. "How could the likes of me sit all day looking at test tubes and running calcula-tions?" So lawyering, whatever lawyers did, it was.

When Gerry was sixteen, he wandered into the University of Wyoming Law School and found the dean. He asked a few pertinent questions about the profession: "Do I have to take Latin?" and "Do lawyers make a lot of money?" (The answers to which were "No" and

"Some do and some don't," respectively—both of which were acceptable answers for Gerry.) He voluntarily sat for a test designed to measure his suitability for the profession and scored higher than anyone the dean had previously tested.

After earning his bachelor's degree (in English) at UW, Gerry entered the UW Law School as the youngest student in his thirty-member class. At the Law School, Gerry held his own—in the classroom, at least. During a moot court in front of a district judge, Gerry was a self-proclaimed disaster. The judge thought so too, telling him in no uncertain terms he would never become a trial lawyer. "I am doing you a favor by being brutally honest with you," the judge said. "I offer you not the slightest encouragement. You have absolutely no native ability whatever to size up a situation and to act upon it appropriately. If you must stay in the law, and I recommend that you don't, you should confine yourself to office work." Needless to say, Gerry didn't listen.

After *not* studying for the bar exam the second time around (as opposed to his first attempt, when he had devoted months to studying), Gerry passed with flying colors. That obstacle down, he then set about slowly becoming one of the most recognized and successful trial lawyers around. It took a couple of decades for him to go from a wet-behind-the-ears young attorney in Riverton to sharing opinions with Paula Zahn on national television and founding Jackson's Spence Law Firm. Law students across the country today study Gerry's courtroom "tactics," although Gerry still maintains that there are no "tactics"—just the simple fact that he never really learned how to ask a proper question and that he tells juries his clients' stories in the language of working people. It's law, Wyoming style.

Reinventing the Log Cabin, as Well as Van Gogh and Elvis
Jackson Hole

The world's most unique log cabin used to sit in a mobile home park on Highway 390. Driving past, motorists would inevitably do a double take: a log cabin in the midst of all these mobile homes? With Elvis peeking out of one window? And a plastic pink flamingo stuck in the front garden? If confounded drivers slowed down and took a closer look, they could see that it was fake, albeit a pretty convincing fake.

Artist Greta Gretzinger had taken a regular, old trailer and painted it to look like a log cabin, complete with Elvis looking out a window and a garden sporting a plastic pink flamingo. That was the side facing the highway. The side facing her neighbors was painted with a mountain

There's Elvis!

mural. "I thought it would be nice if they had a view of mountains when they looked out their windows," Greta explains. This log cabin look was the trailer's second facade. Previously it had been painted with palm trees and flamingos. "After a few years of that I thought it needed a new look, so I went for the log cabin," says Greta, who gave the trailer its log cabin paint job in 1992. She lived in the painted trailer, including its time as both a palm oasis and a log cabin, for fourteen years before selling it. Several years after she moved out, the trailer was torn down to make way for an affordable housing development. The rumor is that the trailer's last owner somehow took the painted Elvis with him. "It makes me happy to think Elvis is still out there somewhere," says Greta.

Even though the trailer is gone, Greta's whimsical art can still be found elsewhere around town. At Pearl Street Bagels, 145 West Pearl Avenue, Greta painted bagel-themed versions of Van Gogh's *The Starry Night* and da Vinci's *Mona Lisa*. In the alleyway between the Sundance Inn and the Ranch Shops in downtown Jackson, she painted a giant landscape mural. "Guests at the motel can look out at scenery rather than blank cinderblock walls." She also has a mural, her interpretation of a famous Albert Bierstadt painting, on an outside wall of the Gun Barrel restaurant as well as interior murals in the Merry Piglets Mexican restaurant. Greta doesn't just work with paint, though. In a private collection in town is another portrait of Elvis, for which she used kidney and black beans, lentils, and dried peas.

The Original eBay
Jackson Hole

Looking to offload your collection of salt-and-pepper shakers or give away a pink shag area rug? Or maybe you're looking for a taxidermied moose, a ride to Salt Lake City, an elk-antler chandelier, or a cat. Perhaps your needs are totally pedestrian: a futon or a used car. Whenever locals here are looking to buy or sell, they can do it for free on Jackson Hole's answer to eBay, the radio program *Trash and Treasure,* which airs on KMTN 96.9 FM from 9:30 to 9:50 A.M. Monday through Saturday. All of the examples above came from a week of shows last summer.

Trash and Treasure has been around long enough to be eBay's grandfather. Deejay Mark "Fish" Fishman has hosted the show (except on Saturday) since 1996. There were several hosts before him. Aside from Fish's voice, every show is different. Since the radio station has gotten a caller-ID system, the prank callers have disappeared (the station doesn't run on much of a delay, so prank calls used to really spice things up). But who needs prank calls when legitimate callers are on air trying to sell their pet iguana? One thing you can't sell on *Trash and Treasure,* though—automatic weapons.

Happy shopping.

Sweet Dreams
Kelly

If my name were plain, old Sheep Mountain, I'd do something, too. Hundreds of millions of years ago, when the Gros Ventre (pronounced "gro vont" in good cowboy French) Mountains were first formed, the rock pile that was Sheep Mountain arranged itself in such a way that it, quite obviously, resembled a sleeping Indian. The 11,239-foot peak is one of the most prominent non-Teton mountains in Jackson Hole, but you'd be hard-pressed to find someone who knows it by anything other than Sleeping Indian.

This might be a little like telling someone what to look for in an optical illusion, but we'll try: From right above the National Elk Refuge outside of Jackson (the best viewing spot), look at the range that isn't the Tetons. The most prominent peak—with jagged cliffs facing Jackson and a long, sloping meadow facing north—is the Sleeping Indian. The jagged cliffs make up his cascading headdress. The big V-notch is his neck, and below that his arms are folded over his chest, which is actually the peak's summit. His legs are stretched out straight below. For a closer view—to actually walk right up his leg, belly, and chest—there is an unmarked trail starting at the National Elk Refuge. The Forest Service in Jackson can tell you where to find it.

Sleeping Indian Mountain, aka Sheep Mountain.

A Mongolian-Inspired Subdivision?

Kelly

Genghis Khan and his Mongolian hordes might have given yurts a bad name (these nomads used them as mobile bases as they swept across the Asian steppes conquering and pillaging all in their path), but not all yurt dwellers are so angry and destructive. A few dozen people live in yurts in Kelly's "Yurtville," and none of their neighbors have ever complained of them conquering or pillaging. There haven't even been murmurs of a yurtie tramping through a vegetable garden.

Invented thousands of years ago by Mongolian nomads, yurts really haven't changed much in their fundamentals. They are circular, lattice-walled, canvas-covered structures that can be quickly set up and taken down, are easy to heat (even in a Wyoming winter), and require no foundation. Today's yurt dwellers have options like French doors, ceiling fans, and skylights to choose from, even though Genghis Khan and his hordes probably didn't. If they had, perhaps they would have spent more time inside and less time striking fear into the hearts of everyone in their path.

Kelly's unique Mongolian-inspired "subdivision."

Slip Sliding Away
Kelly

It's been more than eighty years since the north slope of Sheep Mountain, aka Sleeping Indian, collapsed and sent tons of debris hurtling down its flanks, but the scar is still fresh enough to be seen from miles away. On June 23, 1925, one of the world's largest, fastest-moving landslides happened outside the town of Kelly. In just three minutes, fifty million cubic yards—enough to cover the entirety of Washington, D.C., 6 inches deep—of rock, soil, and other debris slid down from an altitude of 9,000 feet.

The bottom of Sleeping Indian just slid away.

State surveyor W. O. Owen estimated that the builders of the Panama Canal could have gotten their jobs done in fifty-four minutes had they been able to move earth at the speed of the Gros Ventre slide. The debris made its way to the bottom of the mountain, dammed the Gros Ventre River, and continued 400 feet up the opposite slope. This new dam—2,000 feet wide, 1 mile long, and 225 to 250 feet high—on the Gros Ventre created a 5-mile-long lake, Lower Slide Lake.

Although engineers, geologists, and other scientists pronounced this natural dam safe—it was huge, after all—it was breeched in May 1927 and flooded Kelly with 15 feet of water, killing six people and causing massive property damage. The floodwaters were massive enough to wet the streets in Jackson, 12 miles distant.

Despite the collapse of the natural dam, Lower Slide Lake still exists today and is quite nice for kayaking and windsurfing. Just watch out for the standing dead trees—remember, this lake was formerly a forest.

A TRUE FIRST LADY

Wyoming was settled in large part thanks to the Homestead Act of 1862. Wyoming's first homesteader was Mrs. Margaret Dolan, a widow and mother of six. Mrs. Dolan claimed her 160 acres near Egbert.

Cowboy + Chocolate = Dream Come True
Meeteetse

Now, a cowboy in Wyoming—which is the Cowboy State, after all—is about as common as a traffic jam in New York City. Even a rodeo cowboy who doesn't hesitate to jump on the back of a bucking bronc is pretty run-of-the-mill. But a cowboy who funds his rodeo career by making truffles and fancy pastries and cheesecakes? Now that's not your everyday kind of cowboy.

Tim Kellogg was saving for a new bronc saddle a few years ago when his mom recommended he try selling some of his truffles—which he learned to make as a kid while hanging out (and licking the beaters and spatulas) in his grandmother's kitchen—at a summer art fair in Cody. His truffles had always been popular gifts to friends during the holidays, but Tim doubted that anyone would want to buy them, especially in July. How wrong he was—he ended up selling out, and the rest, as they say, is history.

Soon afterward, Tim rented a space in downtown Meeteetse (population: 351), but the shop was open only on Saturday. Two years later, Tim had to rent a bigger space and open seven days a week, rodeo schedule permitting. His truffles—thirty different flavors, including champagne, Irish crème, sage, huckleberry, jalapeño, key lime, cognac, and even Coors (yup, like the beer)—are also available through an online store at www.meeteetsechocolatier.com. If you get a chance to meet him in person—and ladies, he's more than easy on the eyes—his store is in the old Meeteetse Mercantile in downtown Meeteetse. For hours and other information call (307) 868–2567.

It Takes One to Get One
Pinedale

You gotta give it to the Sheepeater Indians (named after their staple diet) for ingenuity. They used bighorn sheep to kill bighorn sheep. The Indians, a branch of the Shoshone, devised a way to make a powerful bow—the most powerful of its time, actually—out of the horns of these sheep. Now, you might have never seen a bighorn sheep up close, but you probably still know that its horns are curled. Quite curled, in fact. The Sheepeater got around this curling, which didn't make for good, true bows, by setting the horns in hot springs or geysers, both of which happen to proliferate in this area. The hot water would cause the horns to become bendable without breaking. The Indians would then straighten the horns out. About two months later, and after many other steps, they had quite an impressive bow: It could shoot an arrow so fast—about 150 feet per second—that the arrow would go completely through a buffalo. The Museum of the Mountain Man (700 East Hennick Street; 877–686–6266) has one of the oldest specimens of this kind of bow. It dates from between 1690 and 1730.

NOT YOUR USUAL WORKDAY

Working cowboy Darrel Winfield was just doing his job at the Quarter Circle Five Ranch outside Pinedale when he was spotted and cast as the iconic Marlboro Man.

Double-Decker
Ralston

You wouldn't expect a town of fewer than fifty residents to have so many bridges, much less one bridge that passes over another, but Ralston does . . . thereby getting itself noticed by *Ripley's Believe It Or Not.* A former railroad siding town, Ralston has a road offering access to Alkali Creek. When the railroad came to town, railroad officials thought that the road had picked a most wonderful spot to cross the river. They built the railroad bridge at the same point. The railroad bridge passes over the highway bridge, and both pass over the creek. Both bridges are still in use today. At least two trains pass over Alkali Creek daily, while fishermen and picnickers take the car bridge down to the banks of the creek. The best view of the bridges, and the access to the river road, is from U.S. Highway 14A, east of Ralston.

The Not-So-Super Superhighway
Smoot

Complaining about the state of the roads in Wyoming is a popular pastime for locals. But really, we have nothing to complain about when we see how far they've come. The country's first-ever federally funded road project west of the Mississippi, the Lander Cutoff—a northern fork of the Oregon Trail that shortened the time to the Pacific by seven days—happens to be right here in Wyoming. The 345-mile Central Division of the Pacific Wagon Road was constructed in 1858 by 115 men. It took a mere ninety days and cost less than $70,000. It makes even today's smallest roads look like superhighways.

If you're really intent on making it to the Pacific in these modern times, you can blast through Wyoming, even on our two-lane state highways, in less than a day. Of course we don't recommend that, but, if you get sick of cowboys, open space, and herds of wildlife, at least you have the option. For early visitors to the area—and as many as 300 wagons and thousands of horses, mules, and cattle traveled the Lander Cutoff daily during its heyday in the 1860s—"blasting through" meant a solid two months . . . and that's counting the seven days saved by taking the cutoff in the first place. But with the rising popularity of cars, this Central Division Road was abandoned.

Today, perhaps hundreds of automobiles travel the highways (mostly U.S. Highways 191 and 351) that bisect the original "road's" remains. Don't look for any sort of crumbled pavement, though. All that's left are wagon-wheel ruts and what very well might be the West's very first potholes. Some of the best viewing is 3 miles south of Smoot on Highway 89. The route of the old Central Division Road actually parallels Highway 89 for about 21 miles through this area.

TALK ABOUT INFLATION

The founder of the Jackson Hole Mountain resort bought the land at the base for $1,350 an acre. A recent real-estate deal is rumored to see a base lot sell for more than $10 million!

Now That's Scary
Teton Village

Evidently space has nothing on Wyoming's biggest ski resort. You know something has to be intimidating when John Glenn, the first American to fly into space, says so. Standing at the top of the Jackson Hole Mountain Resort's famed Corbett's Couloir ski run and looking over its edge, Glenn admitted to a secret fear of heights. Really, it's no wonder, though: The run is nearly vertical at the top and only 40 to 50 feet wide. It does eventually mellow to a mere forty degrees steep. Oh, and I almost forgot: To start, you have to jump between 10 and 15 feet (depending on snow levels) down into it. No one knows whether Glenn jumped into the couloir after suffering from his bit of acrophobia or opted for a mellower line back to the bottom of the mountain.

Standing right in this spot, Astronaut John Glenn developed a fear of heights.

Music for the (Frozen) Masses
Teton Village

In order to make the musician thing work, Peter Chandler has to wear many different hats and play lots of different musical styles, but it's his natural dreadlocks and "ski-bum music" that are most popular. A minister by training (Harvard Divinity School), Peter serves God and skiers

The colder it gets, the harder the Tram Jam Band play.

alike with original ski-bum music. Lyrics include "When I grow up I wanna be a ski bum. Don't you know that's what I want to do? Sitting on the sundeck when it's all said and done with a little snow bunny named Sue." During the ski season, he heads the Tram Jam Band from 11:00 A.M. to 2:00 P.M. on Saturday at the base of the Jackson Hole Mountain Resort. Over the band's ten years, they've played in blizzards, subzero temperatures (the record is twelve degrees below zero), and sleet. "When it's cold and snowy, it's more 'A' for effort than good music," Peter says.

Peter, known as Chan-Man when doing the ski-bum music thing, has been an area fixture for years, but he has been making music even longer. Peter's weirdest night picking the strings happened in a Maine biker bar when he was thirty-two. "We were up there playing blues and this guy asked me to play 'Pretty Woman.' I thought I was too cool and said 'No.' The guy hauls a gun out, points it at me, and says, 'Play "Pretty Woman."' I haven't played it since, but I've learned to fake a lot of songs for a tip."

Staying away from "Pretty Woman" these days, Peter's most famous song is about coffee. "The Coffee Song" is played by ski-bum-sympathetic DJs on lower-wattage stations up and down the Rockies. While writing it, Peter walked into the local grocery store and wrote down the names of all the different coffees, assembling them into a kind of puzzle so they'd work in the song. Sample lyric: "Kona Blend, Sumatra Mandolin, Irish Crème, Cinnamon Hazelnut, Amaretto, Italian Gold, we got Kahlua Fudge, Mississippi Mud, Mocha Java, French Vanilla, Vienna Roast, Organic Nicaraguan . . . "

Turns out "The Coffee Song" was good training for the title track of his band Waist Deep's first album. The newer song has Peter singing, nearly without pause, the names of almost every run at the Jackson Hole Mountain Resort: "Hoback, Jackson Face, Green River, Rock Springs, Cody Bowl, Four Shadows, Four Pines, Thunder Woods, Headwall,

Cirque, Ten Sleep, Amphitheater, Paintbrush, Elevator, Expert Chutes, Twice Is Nice . . . " The list goes on for more than seven minutes.

Peter's tongue isn't the only limber part of his body. He's a former professional footbagger (aka hacky sacker). For his second solo album, *Gotta Take Some Turns*, Peter wrote "Footbag Fever." The song was included in a World Footbag Association instructional video. Darryl Miller used the whole album in the ski flick *Whoopi*.

Cool Chariots
Thayne

In the early 1900s, when the average January could see 10 feet of snow and SUVs and four-wheel drive had yet to be invented, horse-drawn sleighs were often the primary mode of winter transportation in this part of Wyoming. No one really knows who first got the improbable idea to spice things up by trading a sleigh's snow runners for wheels, but it was well before Charlton Heston and Ben Hur made chariot racing cool again. In fact, the first recorded race using such a contraption was in the 1920s. If local rumors can be believed, the first race had a Mormon bishop beating a local rancher down Thayne's iced-over main street.

Despite being perhaps one of the world's first true extreme sports—traveling over an icy track behind two horses pounding at speeds of up to 50 mph is nothing if not extreme—cutter racing most likely won't gain a tremendously wide audience. Its popularity in the West, however, has grown over the years, and Thayne hosted the world's first Cutter and Chariot Racing Championship in 1965. You can catch cutter action in Star Valley from the first weekend in November through March. Phone (307) 883–2759 for details.

Back to Basics . . . Way, Way Back to Basics

Thermopolis

Mammoths, mastodons, and long-horned bison haven't been seen on Wyoming's plains since the last Ice Age—that'd be about 11,000 years ago for those a little fuzzy on their Ice Ages. Such a small detail doesn't stop Thermopolis from hosting an annual competition in which modern man tests his—we can't imagine why most of the competitors here are male—skill with Ice Age–era hunting weapons. At the Foothill-Mountain Atlatl Competition, usually held in early July, you can watch competitors "hunt" (the prey is usually plastic or wooden targets) with bow, spear, knife, hawk, and the über-ancient atlatl (pronounced either AT-ul-LA-tul or AT-lat-ul). Despite its benign appearance, atlatls can hurl darts capable of mortally wounding a mammoth (if one happened to be around) from a distance of nearly 100 yards. Watch out!

Some Like It Hot . . . or Not

Thermopolis

Today, Hot Springs State Park—home of the "World's Largest Mineral Hot Springs," if you are to believe the giant stone letters on the butte above town—is the most popular in the Wyoming State Park system. At the turn of the last century, however, the park, along with the rest of the land in Hot Springs County, was deemed "unwanted" by already established, neighboring counties. Guess cowboys hadn't yet realized how good a warm soak feels.

Once a part of the Wind River Indian Reservation, the hot springs were sold by Chief Washakie to the United States for $60,000 in 1897. The chief put one caveat on the sale: A portion of the springs always had to be reserved for free public use. (A pageant celebrating this gift from the Shoshone tribe is held annually every first weekend in August.)

While the hot springs were just fine in their natural state, concrete pools and water slides were added, and 3.6 million gallons of mineral-laden, 127-degree water (don't worry, it's cooled before it gets to the pools) flow through them daily. The park is open year-round. You can thank Chief Washakie for the bargain-basement price of admission. For more information on the park, call (307) 864–2176.

The world's largest mineral hot spring in Thermopolis.

Three Waters Mountain
Union Pass

It's pretty difficult to escape the Continental Divide while in Wyoming. It bisects the state in more places than you can count. Believe me, I've tried. On Interstate 80 in the southern part of the state, you'll see CONTINENTAL DIVIDE, ELEV. 7,000 FEET signs. You'll see them in Yellowstone National Park as well. And up on Togowtee Pass. And in the Medicine Bow Mountains. Really, they're everywhere. You'll see so many Continental Divide signs in fact, that the idea—on one side of the sign water flows to the Atlantic and on the other side to the Pacific—will cease to be novel. There are several Continental Divide points, however, that can never cease to be curious. Three Waters Mountain, where three of the continent's seven major watersheds meet (one of only two places in North America where this happens), is at the top of that list.

Imagine a raindrop—let's make it a big raindrop—landing somewhere along the 4-mile crest of this 11,675-foot peak. It actually splits into thirds, with the three tiny driblets wending their separate ways to three different major bodies of water: the Gulf of California (the drop travels 1,300 miles), the Pacific (a 1,400-mile trip), and the Gulf of Mexico (3,000 miles distant).

Slightly less ambitious raindrops land a few miles away, at Parting of the Waters Natural Landmark near Togowtee Pass. Here, North Two Ocean Creek flows down from a plateau and hits the summit ridge of Two Ocean Pass, one of Wyoming's many, many segments of the Continental Divide. Upon hitting this ridge, the creek actually splits into two, sending some of its water down each side of the Divide. The two splitter creeks are aptly named: Atlantic Creek and Pacific Creek. Go ahead: Stand right at the fork and ponder that the water rushing past one of your feet is headed to the Pacific and the water wetting the other foot is en route to the Atlantic.

The Never-Ending House
Wapiti

There is no doubt about it: Wyoming is the land of the log cabin. Driving west from Cody toward Yellowstone National Park—a stretch of road that President Teddy Roosevelt once called the most beautiful in the world—you'll see cute log cabins. And then you'll see George "Lee" Smith's log "lodge," for lack of a better word.

Smith began construction sometime in the early 1970s and worked on his four-story-plus-a-crow's-nest creation until the day he died in April 1992. An architect, he used the house to experiment with all sorts of styles and materials. Every part of the house is made from reclaimed material or giant logs that Lee and his wife at the time, Linda, cut and hauled down from nearby Rattlesnake Mountain. Lee briefly lived in the house, but he never did get around to installing water or electricity.

Actually, there are lots of things he never got around to installing, such as an elevator from the old Western Wear store in Cody that was to be the only internal access to the upper floors (there are exterior stairs on the house). And there's beautiful maple flooring Lee plucked piece by piece out of the Meeteetse school gym that was never laid down. Linda says that she doubts the house would ever have been finished, even if Lee had lived. "It was his art project. He was always finding new scrap materials that were salvageable and that he wanted to use," she says.

Lee didn't work just with materials he brought to the site; he also worked with what was at the site. Because the land underneath the house is an old glacier tip, the ground is littered with rocks. Unable—or not wanting to?—dig up one of the largest boulders, Lee just built the house around it. If you walk into the first floor, it's the first thing you see.

Even as a work in progress, this house is an architectural wonder.

Now owned by Lee and Linda's daughter, the home has fallen into disrepair. Local teens use it for parties. Linda says she would love to see the house restored and finished, but "that would take more money than God has. It'd be a wonderful project for someone with lots of money, though."

Build It and They Might Not Come
Wapiti

The advertisement was daunting: "Must be able to take care of himself and his horses under very trying conditions, build trails and cabins, ride all day and night. Pack, shoot and fight fire without losing his head. All this requires a very vigorous constitution . . . the hardest kind of physical work from beginning to end."

So read the ad for Forest Service rangers in the early 1900s. Today, you can see the building that was the very first Forest Service headquarters in the country and where the men who possessed the ad's qualifications lived and worked. Thankfully, to visit it, you don't even need to know how to build a trail or a cabin—much less shoot and fight fires without losing your head. Built in 1903, the log building has been slightly remodeled and expanded to meet the needs of today's Forest Service. Stop in to get the latest information on hiking trails, wildfires, and bear warnings or to reserve a campsite.

And You Think You're Old
Washakie Wilderness, Double Cabin Trailhead

After covering 28 miles of dirt road to get to this trailhead, you're going to wish it was your butt that was petrified and not the trees you've come to see. Thirty to forty million years ago, the forest around here was a bucolic, fecund area with abundant flora and fauna. Then massive volcanic ash deposits rained down. Most everything was killed, but before some of the trees had a chance to rot, their wood cells were replaced by minerals and water and they petrified. And here they have remained ever since.

Although petrified, pieces of the trees do break off, but it's illegal to take them from inside wilderness boundaries. For the first mile or so of the Frontier Creek Trail, which is the trail you take to get to the petrified forest, you are not in wilderness, so you are allowed to pick up pieces of tree rock that have been washed down the creek. The trailhead is about 40 miles north of Dubois. For more detailed directions call the Shoshone National Forest Ranger Station at (307) 455–2466.

NO CHILD LEFT BEHIND

Wyoming would be among the first states in the country to have a tax-supported public school system, except that it wasn't yet a state when the legislature passed the first school law in 1869. In 1873, again before it was a state, Wyoming stressed that all schools should teach the same material and that all teachers should receive the same training.

93

Given Time, Anything Can Change
Wilson

"You have the privilege tonight of hearing the worst country western band in the U.S.," Bill Briggs used to tell the crowd gathered to dance at the Stagecoach Bar in Wilson every Sunday night. He was talking about his own Stagecoach Band. Bill was being modest, though. Twenty or so years ago, *Skiing Magazine* actually named the band "the worst country western band in the western hemisphere." "We were such hackers," says Bill, who has played with the band almost from the beginning and took over managerial duties in the late 1980s.

Today, thirty-eight years after having first taken the stage and missing only those Sunday nights that happened to coincide with New Year's Eve and Christmas, the Stagecoach Band is famous, but no longer for their awfulness. Everyone from grizzled cowboys to former Olympians makes room in their schedules for dancing Sunday night at the Stagecoach. The band still doesn't practice, though.

It all started on February 16, 1969. The Coach, as it's known in these parts, wasn't the kind of bar that welcomed outsiders, especially ones bearing instruments. There certainly wasn't a dance floor, or even a jukebox. There were fights most nights. A few musicians in town wanted to make music badly enough that they were willing to brave the rough-and-tough Coach crowds. They were also optimistic that their performances might mellow out the bar's scene a bit.

Early on, the band was paid with free drinks and performed without amplification and over the din of the crowd. Actually, the band had an amplifier, but it was old and had been stored in a barn. Its insides were a mess of dust and pigeon poop. By 1972, having gotten to the point where their presence was at least accepted by the crowd—although no one had yet seen fit to dance to any of the music the band played—and sick of losing their voices every Sunday night, band members finally convinced the bar's owner to invest in something better. It was only after the arrival of real amps and microphones that the Sunday-night dance scene the Coach is now known for first got going. Not that the dancers seemed to care, but it was a few years after the amps' arrival that *Skiing Magazine* called the band's disorganization and lack of talent to national attention. The band just kept on playing, though, somewhat reveling in the magazine's pronouncement.

Nowadays, the band is as strong as ever. They will play their 2,000th performance in August 2007. (The band has missed only three Sundays over the years; the Stagecoach Bar is closed on Christmas, so when that holiday falls on a Sunday, even though the Stagecoach Band is ready and willing to play, they can't.) There's a roster of more than twenty area musicians to choose from. The band's first second-generation member joined a little over five years ago. Bob Dylan, Tom Paxton, and Jerry Jeff Walker have all joined the band on stage. (Dylan, however, joined the band not at the Coach but rather when they were playing at a local wedding at which he was a bored guest.) "As you get a reputation, people want to say that they have played with you," Bill says. Cynics might ask, "A reputation for what?" but most people are too busy twirling around the dance floor to listen. Who knew bad music could end up being so good?

The Stagecoach Bar is at the base of Teton Pass in Wilson. For information call (307) 733–4407.

M. C. Escher Meets Wyoming
Wilson

Metal sculptor John Simms didn't know what he was going to do with the six semicircles, each with a 7-foot radius, that he had picked up at a salvage yard in Idaho Falls. Always up for working with nearly anything, however, he saw potential. But potential for what? Three 14-foot-diameter full circles?

John arranged and rearranged the pieces—which wasn't easy considering they weighed about 200 pounds each—until finally his arms and back were screaming for relief. John recreated the six pieces in miniature—the minis had a radius of only 1 foot—

John Simms's bison sculpture—can you see it?

and again began to play around with different arrangements. He would assemble the pieces flat in his driveway and then ascend a stepladder to look down and see if it worked. Nothing seemed to work, however. And then suddenly, without even trying to consciously create any recognizable form—he had initially been going for something abstract—a recognizable form was born. Recognizable to John, at least. After finding this form, John scrapped the minis and went big. A 12-foot-tall and 18-foot-long form was installed on Teton Village Road for all passersby to see.

"About 90 percent of people can see that it is a bison, but 10 percent don't get it at all. Maybe half of the 10 percent get it when someone points it out," John says. "The rest are totally clueless no matter what you do. I didn't mean for it to be any kind of illusion; this just shows how funny our minds can be."

A Trip Back in Time
Wind River Canyon

It's only 12 miles of road, but it covers three billion years and two rivers. And it includes an optical illusion courtesy of Mother Nature: If you don't look carefully, you'll think the Wind River actually flows upstream!

But let's start at the beginning, well before the concept of an optical illusion had been thought up. Well before, well, *anything* had been thought up, actually. Within the 2,000-foot-deep Wind River canyon lie some of the oldest exposed rocks in the world. Here, you can check out—and even get out of your car and touch—rocks from every formation of each major era of the earth's development: variegated rocks of the Eocene Wind River formation; severely faulted Paleozoic rocks; Precambrian crystalline rocks; Cambrian shales; Triassic red beds. Thankfully, the state of Wyoming has assumed that few of us can tell the difference between Eocene variegation and garden stones and has labeled the canyon with interpretative signs.

Before exiting the canyon into Thermopolis, check out the two-rivers-in-one at Wedding of the Waters. You will already have noticed that it is indeed only one river that runs through the Wind River Canyon, the predictably named Wind River, but ½ mile before Thermopolis, it becomes (!) the Bighorn River. In 1803 Lewis and Clark, traveling farther north and east, named this river the Bighorn. But the Crow Indians, who lived near the river's headwaters, had already named it the Wind River. Both names were in wide use before settlers realized that the Bighorn River and the Wind River were actually one and the same. In a bit of diplomatic compromising that would have made our Founding Fathers proud, it was decided that the river would keep both names: Below the Wedding of the Waters, it is the Bighorn; above the Wedding of the Waters, it is the Wind River. "Wedding of the Waters"—not a bad way to cover up a big boo-boo.

See billions of years over just a few miles.

No Tall Tales Necessary
Yellowstone National Park

Fishermen are famous for their tall tales, but only the sorriest of their numbers should have to make exaggerated excuses for not catching anything here. Counting all the park's lakes, creeks, and streams, there are more than 400 different bodies of water—2,650 miles of rivers and streams and 120 lakes—on which to fish. Yellowstone Lake's surface area of 136 square miles makes it the largest high-altitude lake in North America. Within these waters is the world's largest inland population of cutthroat trout. Shoshone Lake, accessible only by hiking or horseback riding, is the largest backcountry lake in the lower forty-eight states. The park has the last major undammed river (the 671-mile-long Yellowstone River) in the lower forty-eight states.

Fly fishing is usually catch-and-release, but at this lakeside geyser it's hook-and-cook.

If these numbers alone aren't enough to get an angler's confidence up, consider this: Not only are Yellowstone's fish plentiful, but plenty of them are also pretty stupid. Fish in backcountry spots, which is much of what Yellowstone waters are, rarely see fishermen. That means the fish haven't had much of a chance to learn the difference between a hook and a legitimate lunch. Some of them are so stupid that you don't even need a rod to catch them; you can "tickle" them right into your creel. Tickler-type fishermen forgo rods for bare hands, holding a hand underwater until a fish swims lazily by. When the fish swims over their hand, they brush the fish's belly with a finger. Evidently, the fish likes this tickling and sticks around for more belly brushing. Before the fish knows it, it's been lulled right into a creel. However, if you end up catching a fish in this manner, be sure to get some pictures, 'cause tickling sounds like a tall tale of the most embellished kind.

Even though no longer allowed, there's another wacky type of fishing that used to be practiced on the shores of Yellowstone Lake. In 1870 a member of the Washburn Party, one of the earliest groups of whites to explore and document the wonders of what was to become Yellowstone, watched as a fisherman's catch accidentally slipped into a thermal cone on the shores of Yellowstone Lake. The fisherman fished his catch out, only to find that it had been boiled and was suitable for eating. Because of changing water levels in the lake, Fishing Cone Geyser is no longer hot enough for an impromptu fish fry.

A MOUNTAIN WITH A STORY TO TELL

If you hear screaming around Roaring Mountain in Yellowstone National Park, you're not going crazy. Nor are you hearing a person in trouble. The mountain itself is the one doing the talking. Explorers as far back as 1885 noted the "shrill, penetrating sound" of the steam constantly escaping from several vents near the peak's summit. In fact, it's the screaming steam that gave the mountain its name.

ICE HOT

When Yellowstone Lake freezes (it starts to freeze between October and November and remains frozen generally until June), it is one of the biggest ice sheets in the continental United States. But even though the ice is 2 feet thick in spots on top of the lake, places at the bottom remain near boiling because of thermal activity.

Past the Middle of Nowhere
Yellowstone National Park

You'd better make a grocery list when you live at the Thorofare Ranger Cabin. If you forget to get the eggs or sugar, it's not just a long drive back to the store, but also a long walk. A very long walk. The cabin is a 32-mile march from the nearest road. As the crow flies though—if you can find one willing and able to carry you—it's a mere 20 miles.

Tucked into the Yellowstone/Teton Wilderness border, the Thorofare Ranger Cabin sits smack in the middle of the most remote spot in the lower forty-eight states. In this instance, "remote" is defined as the place farthest from a road. Montana has a spot that is 18 miles—again, as the crow flies—from a road. It is 16 air miles to get to the lower forty-eight states' third most remote spot. Neither the second- nor third-place spots have anyone living in them, though. Yellowstone backcountry rangers have stayed in the spartan Thorofare Cabin, venturing out to the road only a few times each summer, since it was built decades ago. (The cabin is only occupied during the summer.) One ranger, Bob Jackson, called the cabin home for nearly twenty-five summers. When not at the cabin, Jackson lived a relatively cosmopolitan life: He had a road that went right by his driveway at a South Dakota ranch.

DOING THINGS BACKWARD

Some lakes are just so predictable—their waters flow through a series of rivers, creeks, and streams and empty into a single ocean. Isa Lake, at an altitude of 8,262 feet and 7 miles south of Yellowstone National Park's Old Faithful on the Grand Loop Road, throws convention to the wind. Not only does Isa Lake drain into both the Atlantic and Pacific Oceans, but it does so backwards! The lake's western half heads east via the Firehole, Madison, Missouri, and Mississippi Rivers until it dumps into the Gulf of Mexico. The water draining from the eastern part of the lake goes west and ends up in the Pacific by way of the Lewis, Snake, and Columbia Rivers. Who knew a lake could be so confused?

KEEP THE CHANGE

Morning Glory pool, the second most visited thermal feature in Yellowstone National Park, used to be so hot that no algae could grow in it. Its crystal-clear waters perfectly reflected the sky. But then tourists started to throw things into it, as though it were a fountain. These items clogged the vent at the pool's bottom and caused the water temperature to drop enough that algae began to grow. Algae-covered water couldn't reflect the sky.

In the 1950s park rangers decided to clean Morning Glory. They lowered the pool's water level, and the spring at the bottom actually erupted as a geyser. It wasn't just water that came flying out, though: The pool puked up $86.27 in pennies, $8.10 in other change, tax tokens from nine states, seventy-six handkerchiefs, and logs, bottles, tin cans, towels, socks, shirts, and underwear.

Another park geyser regurgitated even odder contents. In 1948 everything from a frying pan to bath mats, a kerosene lamp, marbles, a lightbulb, a broom, raincoats, bricks, and cake molds were pulled from Thud Geyser.

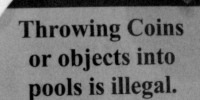

Update

Throwing Coins or objects into pools is illegal.

The fine for throwing things in hot springs is $100
Report violations to a Park Ranger or call
(307) 344-7381.
<u>Why is it illegal to throw things in hot springs?</u>

❦ **The coins will build up with silica and eventually can plug and kill geysers and hot springs.**

❦ **Park rangers have to risk their lives, standing next to boiling waters, to get trash out of them.**

❦ **Please help protect Yellowstone and keep America's 1st National Park beautiful. Thank you!**

It's tempting, but don't do it.

As It Was

Yellowstone National Park

Want to play explorer, imagining yourself back in the days when it was only Native Americans and fur trappers out here? Well, then, you should head into Yellowstone. While there are obviously some buildings and roads, development has been kept to a minimum. Less than 2 percent of the total land—and Yellowstone is bigger than Rhode Island and Delaware combined—has been developed. The park has four times as many miles of backcountry trails (1,200 miles) as it does miles of road. Although the 300 miles of pavement might be crowded, only 2 percent of the annual three million or so visitors to Yellowstone ever make it more than 100 yards from the road.

You can escape into the backcountry and not see another soul for days. You will see the only place in the lower forty-eight states that still has all of it native species of animals. Although wolves were hunted and poisoned to extinction in the 1930s—they were considered varmints, and the government actually paid bounties for them—*canis lupus* brought down from Canada were reintroduced here in 1995 (fourteen wolves) and 1996 (seventeen wolves). In the years since, they have multiplied to more than 300, about 250 of which live in the park itself. (In case you're wondering, the rest live in national forests and wilderness lands surrounding the park.)

With the reintroduction of wolves, Yellowstone's animal life returned to exactly as it was when John Colter, the first white man to explore the area, passed though. A total of 398 different animals now live in the park. Had Columbus arrived in Yellowstone instead of the Bahamas (let's not concern ourselves with the fact that there is no way he could have sailed to Wyoming—use your imagination) he would have found exactly the same animals that are here now. Not only is Yellowstone's native animal population intact, but the park contains the greatest number of wild animals living in their natural habitat in the country.

Sometimes Overdue Can Be Good
Yellowstone National Park

If Yellowstone is supposed to be one of the world's most volcanic areas, then where are the volcanoes? Look down. Almost anywhere you stand in Yellowstone National Park is on (or, more correctly, in) the volcano. Yellowstone's volcano is so huge—one of the few "supervolcanoes" in the world—that nearly the entire national park is contained within its caldera. It is big enough that the entire city of Tokyo could fit inside.

As far as scientists can tell, Yellowstone has exploded three times over the years. The first explosion was 2.1 million years ago; the second eruption happened 1.3 million years ago; and the most recent was 640,000 years ago. If, looking at these dates, you've noticed a trend of an explosion every 600,000 years or so, you're right . . . which means Yellowstone is about 40,000 years overdue for its next eruption. And there's no chance it could have happened without the scientists noticing it. When the Yellowstone volcano explodes, it will be the 1980 Mount St. Helens eruption times 2,500. The last eruption blanketed most of the United States east of here with ash.

The last supervolcano to erupt was Sumatra's Toba 74,000 years ago. Climatologists have learned that Toba sent so much ash and sulfur dioxide into the stratosphere that it blocked out the sun, causing the planet's temperature to drop drastically and possibly reducing the planet's human population to only a few thousand people. Volcanologists say a Yellowstone eruption would be even larger.

Before you hop in your car and quickly get as far away from here as possible, know that even though Yellowstone is running late, scientists say there are few indications that it's going to be doing anything over the next several thousand years. These same scientists have calculated that the movement of magma beneath Yellowstone has caused the ground in some parts of the park to rise an estimated 70 centimeters over the last century. For comparison, that's about the same rate as fingernails grow. That certainly makes it sounds like something is going on down there.

Periodically, engineer types come up with proposals to safely remove the buildup of gases in Yellowstone's magma chamber. While drilling holes or using explosives to release small amounts (that is, non-catastrophic levels) of pressure in a controlled manner sounds reasonable, such actions could actually trigger an eruption. I don't know about you, but I'd say we should just let sleeping magma lie.

MAN VERSUS NATURE

More firefighters were called in to fight the 1988 Yellowstone fires than had ever before been assembled in one place. In total, 9,400 firefighters—a number nearly equal to one-fifth of the population of Wyoming's largest city—were brought to Yellowstone from around the country. By the time all the fires were extinguished in October (an effort that cost $120 million), an area equal in size to Delaware had burned inside the park.

CENTRAL

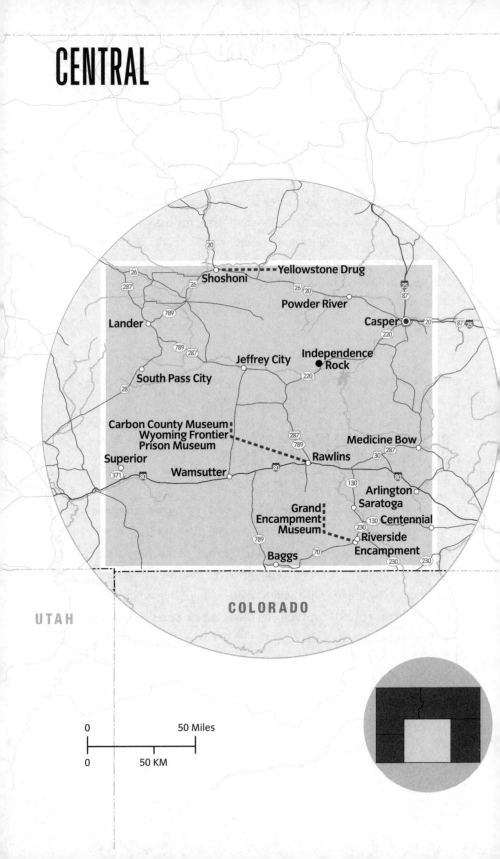

Yellowstone Drug

Shoshoni

Powder River

Lander

Casper

South Pass City

Jeffrey City

Independence Rock

Carbon County Museum
Wyoming Frontier
Prison Museum

Medicine Bow

Superior

Wamsutter

Rawlins

Arlington
Saratoga

Grand
Encampment
Museum

Centennial

Riverside
Encampment

Baggs

COLORADO

UTAH

0   50 Miles

0   50 KM

CENTRAL

Some people—and really, I don't know who these quick-to-judge people would be—say that central Wyoming is the reason the state should abolish its speed limit. Sure, its vast, desertlike expanses, viewed while screaming along Interstate 80 at 80 miles per hour, do seem a bit boring, but that idea only lasts until you see your first desert elk or 12-foot-tall sage tree. By the time you've ogled the only handpainted dance floor west of the Mississippi (and perhaps the only dance floor painted by a colorblind artist) and survived the gas chamber in Rawlins, you're likely to be looking to relocate here. Don't make up your mind too quickly, though. Pedro Mountain has a pygmy demon who, despite its ominous-sounding name, wouldn't make for a bad neighbor. And you can never live too close to the only pair of shoes in the world made both by and from man.

Don't Judge a Book by Its Cover
I–80 Corridor

The land here looks about as barren as barren can get, yet it is actually rife with life. Wyoming has thirteen different species of sagebrush—not that they're easily identifiable by the average nonbotanist layperson—and this area is home to nearly all of them. But the sage is only the beginning. More than 200 species of animals and other plants depend on Wyoming's sage: eighty-seven types of mammals, ninety-four types of birds, sixteen types of Indian paintbrushes, twenty-four types of lichens, thirty-one types of fungi, thirty-two types of midges, fifty-two types of aphids, seventy-four types of spiders, twelve types of katydids, and twelve types of grasshoppers. Included in these numbers are one of the world's few herds of desert elk and the world's largest populations of sage grouse and pronghorn antelope (more than 500,000 in case you're wondering). Not even a mature forest has this much diversity of species.

Even though the United States has 150 million acres of sagebrush, it isn't all as fecund as the stuff here. Because of overgrazing, there are actually very few healthy sagebrush ecosystems. The sage system here, however, is so robust that some of the "bushes" grow to be 12 feet tall. Six feet is more usual, though . . . but that's still tall enough to prove that looks, especially while traveling at 75 mph on the interstate, can indeed be deceiving.

I-80 corridor.

HISTORICALLY SIGNIFICANT OR NOT

I don't know who has kept track of this historical tidbit, but Arlington is where white men first burned coal.

Somewhere, a Beach Is Missing All of Its Sand
Arlington

When attempting to set the world record for the biggest sandcastle, sand architects spent a week in Myrtle Beach, South Carolina, hauling, pushing, and shaping two million pounds of sand. They could have done it a lot faster had they enlisted the help of the Wyoming Department of Transportation (WYDOT). When the 45-mile stretch of I–80 between Arlington and Walcott Junction is hit with a big snowstorm, WYDOT works with that much sand in forty-eight hours. And WYDOT never has a chance to get out of practice: This being Wyoming, a big snowstorm can happen any month of the year. All this sand—up to 1,000 tons in a twenty-four-hour period—is required, even though this same expanse of road is home to more snow fence (40,000 feet, in fact) than anywhere else in the state.

Even with sand and snow fence, this is the most treacherous stretch of road in the state. In the early 1970s an article in a Rawlins newspaper christened it the "Snow Chi Min Trail."

Rumor has it that it's the most often closed section of I–80 in the country (my bet is that it might be tied with the stretch over Donner Pass in California); it can be closed for anywhere from a few hours to a few days.

WYDOT doesn't always get it closed in time, though. Bill Sherwood, a WYDOT employee for more than twenty years, says he once pulled up behind a car stuck in a snowdrift off the road. The wind was blowing, and visibility was spotty, at best. Bill waited for a break in the wind and whiteout conditions; when that break finally came, he got out of his car to check on the stuck vehicle. He walked right up to the driver's window and saw the driver staring intently ahead. Bill noticed that the car's wheels were still spinning. He knocked on the window. The driver jumped and screamed. Visibility was so bad that he had had no idea he was stuck sideways in a drift; he thought he was still driving straight down the highway.

Obviously a few more million pounds of sand are needed.

DOING IT SOLO

Whether it was because Wyoming generally likes to be left alone or because it is so far from Wall Street, Wyoming was the last state to request federal financial aid during the Great Depression.

Outlaws Partied Here
Baggs

Baggs lies 60 or so miles from I–80 and even farther from the nearest town with a population of more than a few hundred. But if you think the town is isolated today, it was even more so in the 1880s and 1890s. That made it just perfect for the likes of Butch Cassidy, the Sundance Kid, and the rest of the Wild Bunch. The gang would often come to Baggs to celebrate their latest heist, holing up in a boardinghouse/dance hall that still stands in the center of town. Nearly as skilled with a harmonica as with a gun, Butch evidently was often the house's entertainment. Even though he reportedly died in 1909 in Bolivia, Baggs residents have insisted that Butch was here hunting with friends in 1929 and 1930. The Gaddis Matthews House is on Main Street (Highway 789) in downtown Baggs.

GOLDEN CHICKEN

From 1865 to 1880 plenty of gold was extracted from the hills in and around South Pass City and Atlantic City. Mines were dug, sluiceways were built (although not always successfully), and the miners endured many hardships and privations. The gold business wasn't always so difficult, though. In 1928 a butcher just doing his job in a Casper meat market struck it rich. Or at least temporarily rich. While cutting up a chicken sold to him by an area chicken farm, the butcher discovered a wheat-grain-size gold nugget inside the bird. Word of his find got out, and soon the chicken farm was overrun by fortune seekers. Unfortunately, no lodes were found. No one knows what the butcher did with his prize.

CENTRAL

Antigravity
Casper

I wonder if NASA knows about this. There's a downhill dip on the road up Casper Mountain where you can stop and put your car in neutral without worrying. Not only will your car not start screaming, out of control, the rest of the way downhill, but it will actually roll backward, uphill. This is no optical illusion. There's no missing that the tail end of your car is higher than the front end; forward is downhill, and backward is uphill. Your car will roll uphill, against gravity, for a decent enough distance to leave you and any other occupants completely bewildered.

To experience this gravitational wonder, take Walcott toward the mountains and turn onto Garden Creek Road. About ½ mile up the road, you'll see a tree standing by itself on the right-hand side. Pull out of the main flow of traffic and put your car in neutral there. By the time the goofy gravity is finished with you, you'll find yourself almost back to the point where you turned onto Garden Creek Road.

FAMILY HISTORY

Outlaw Butch Cassidy was sent to jail by William Simpson, grandfather of Alan Simpson, who served as a Wyoming senator from 1979 to 1997.

Prehistoric Picassos
Castle Gardens

The word went out like wildfire: "Whoever stole it had better return it to the proper authorities—or risk getting both legs broken." What theft would incite the residents and ranchers in and around Riverton to threaten such vigilante violence? It wasn't their life savings stolen from the local bank but rather an ancient artwork . . . of a snapping turtle.

It might have been the castlelike appearance of the rock here, complete with towers and turrets, that gave this area its name, but it is the numerous unique millennium-old petroglyphs that draw scholars, archaeologists, and thieves to Castle Gardens from around the world. In 1940 the state of Wyoming had sent photographer Ted Sowers here to capture the area's most interesting petroglyph, the Great Turtle Shield, on film. Sowers arrived only to find that vandals had chiseled the intricate, four-color turtle out of the rock. All that remained of the turtle was a gaping hole in the rock. After news of this petroglyph pilfering got out, locals issued their ultimatum: Return the turtle or get your gams broke. Not surprisingly,

Where's the turtle?

the turtle showed up. On September 20, 1941, it was anonymously donated to the Wyoming State Museum in Cheyenne.

Castle Gardens is between Lander and Riverton. For directions on how to get there in your four-wheel-drive car, stop in at the Lander Office of the Bureau of Land Management or call (307) 332–8400.

The turtle without his rock neighbors.

Diligent Policing
Centennial

Centennial's police force hasn't taken a day off since its establishment in 1979. Neither has it really moved. An unincorporated town, Centennial doesn't actually have its own police "force"; it has a single car. With coffee cans on its roof to approximate flashers. And a barely-believable-even-from-a-great-distance paint job. And no windows. The car, a 1958 Ford Fairlane, was mobile once, but no one can remember when that might have been.

In 1979 a group of heavily caffeinated and bored Centennial locals got the idea to help out the good deputies of the Albany County Sheriff's Office, the agency tasked with policing their town. Noticing there was a wrecked car sitting off the side of a road outside of town, the group of men (of course!) painted the junker to look like a patrol car and put coffee cans on top to mimic a real cop-car's flashers. They moved the car, a 1950s Plymouth with tailfins, to a prominent place in town along Highway 130. It sat there, unmolested and deterring no one from speeding, until the early 1990s, when a different group of locals decided the "force" needed to be upgraded and took it upon themselves to do it. They traded the Plymouth for the 1958 Fairlane that sits in downtown Centennial today. Hooligans have been less kind to this newer model; none of the windows are intact anymore, and it has been crashed into several times. "The first car, even though it was put out as a joke, might have slowed a few people down, but this one hasn't done anything of the sort," says longtime Centennial resident Murf Serf. "It's still funny, though."

Thinking that the good people of Centennial deserved a better fake police car, the Albany County Sheriff's Office donated an actual retired patrol car to the town in the mid-1990s. There was a problem, though. Since Centennial is an unincorporated town, there is no town government.

The Sheriff's Office didn't know to whom they should give the car. While looking for the proper beneficiary, they parked the car downtown. And, wonder of wonders, it did deter speeders! After a bit of time, it was decided that the local Lions Club should be made responsible for the car, but the Lions were not in agreement among themselves as to what should be done with it. Rumors of infighting over the car trickled through town. The Lions moved the cruiser around town a few times. Then, ostensibly because no one could agree where its permanent home should be, the car ended up parked in a back lot. The Albany County Sheriff's Office eventually came and took it back. Evidently Centennial isn't big enough for two fake cop cars.

BLOWIN' IN THE WIND

Lots of towns in Wyoming claim they have the worst wind in the state. Nowhere but Centennial can claim a wind that was blowing with such persistence and force that it sent a 2x4 right through a truck's tire, completely puncturing the tire. That is exactly what happened to Pat and Nici Self's 1949 Chevy pickup. Nici took a photo of her beleaguered truck and sent it in to *Ripley's Believe It Or Not*. Ripley's recognized Centennial's wind as truly superb.

Census Shenanigans
Centennial

No one in Centennial knows the town's real population anymore. The sign outside town pegs it at one hundred residents, but no one is so foolish as to believe that. A town named Centennial with exactly one hundred residents—what are the chances? And even if Centennial's population was one hundred at one point, what are the chances it has stayed exactly that for nearly thirty years, as the unchanging sign welcoming you to town would indicate?

Up until 1980 Centennial's official population had been fifty for as long as anyone could remember. (It seems that the population signs don't get updated around here too often.) In that year's fateful census, however, it skyrocketed—at least for a population of fifty—doubling to one hundred. It's entirely possible that the population had legitimately reached that grand figure in 1980, but locals rankled a bit, and still rankle a bit, at the idea that they live in such a populous place. You see, Centennialites are generally of the mind that one hundred residents equal a city rather than a small town. And they prefer to live in a small town.

The tale told around Centennial about the town-swelling census is that the census worker, who was a temporary Centennial resident at the time, thought it would be "cute" to have a town named Centennial with one hundred residents. I bet the government thought it would be cute to have the correct population figure.

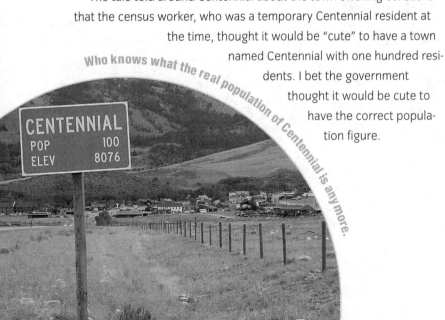

Who knows what the real population of Centennial is anymore.

If you decide to take it upon yourself to figure out exactly what Centennial's population is today and you start driving around town counting people, make sure to notice the odd size of the lots. You'd think lots would be kind of roomy here in the wide and open West, but that's not so in Centennial. The typical lot size is a mere 26 feet wide by a staggering 132 feet long. Having started out as a mining town, the story goes that the miners would pitch their tents in the front of their lots—and tents certainly weren't too wide—and put their mules, and the flies that came with them, as far back as possible.

Not Your Average Gun

Centennial

Wyomingites own guns of all sorts, but West Magoon has a kind of gun that I'm pretty sure can't be found anywhere else in the state. A photographer and potter, West one day found himself inspired not by Mother Nature, a sunset, or even plain practicality but rather by sci-fi superheroes. And so the raku-fired ray gun was born. A longtime science-fiction fan, West originally meant to make a raku ray gun only for himself, but it turned out so well he made more. It was every bit as balanced as a real gun, and the glazes used on raku and the firing process the sculpture goes through

Here's what happens when you're a potter and a sci-fi fan.

Gems-Backfire
West Magoon

resulted in a metallic finish even Flash Gordon would be proud of. Last summer, West sent some of his clay guns to the World Science Fiction Convention in Anaheim, California. Evidently he's not the only person out there who likes both ray guns and raku: A few guns sold.

West and girlfriend Tana's Earthship–style home studio—made from adobe and more than 1,600 tires—is open to visitors who call ahead (307–742–5756).

Ming the Merciless
West Magoon

Martha Stewart meets Star Trek.

CENTRAL

Double-Decker Doody

Encampment

No, the two-story outhouse at the Grand Encampment Museum wasn't designed with practical jokers in mind, but rather was designed for practicality. If you happen into Encampment in the winter, you already know how much snow this area of Wyoming can get. If you're passing through in summer, you'll have to trust me when I say that a typical winter, especially for miners living deep in the surrounding mountains, means several feet of snow on the ground. What, you might ask, does snow have to do with going to the bathroom? Today, the two have nothing to do with each other. But back when thousands of miners lived in these mountains and before indoor plumbing was around, going to the bathroom meant a trip to the outhouse. Having an outhouse buried under snow wasn't good.

Whether the creator of the two-story outhouse was terribly lazy—perhaps he, and there's no doubt it was a he, couldn't stand shoveling the outhouse door out—or terribly inspired, no one knows. The innovation, however, was very much welcomed by mining communities, and various versions of two-story outhouses became ubiquitous in high-altitude/high-snow areas. Miners would do their business on the main floor of the outhouse until the snow got too deep, and then they'd climb upstairs to the second story.

Although we don't think the museum's folding bathtub originally went with the two-story outhouse—miners aren't known as the cleanest bunch—it's worth a look-see as well. So are the remnants of what was once the world's longest aerial tram. In the early twentieth century, the 20-mile tramway stretched from the copper mining town of Rudefeha, where two-story outhouses were most certainly the rage, all the way to the reduction plant in Encampment. The Grand Encampment Museum (807 Barnett; 307–327–5105) is open from late May through September.

PIONEER GRAFFITI

If only there had been spray paint in the mid-1800s, Independence Rock would undoubtedly look very, very different today. Because Edward Seymour didn't invent aerosol paint until 1949, however, the estimated 550,000 pioneers who traveled the Oregon Trail had only crude tools, wagon tar, buffalo grease, and glue to leave their mark on this "Register of the Desert." Given this nickname in 1840, Independence Rock still bears proof of hundreds of passing pioneers.

At one time the twenty-five-acre granite monolith had up to 40,000 names and messages, but erosion and lichen have wiped most away. Since spray paint has been around, it's been illegal to deface or write on the rock with anything, including retro materials like buffalo grease and wagon tar. Independence Rock is between Rawlins and Casper off Highway 220 just next to the middle of nowhere.

Think spray paint would have lasted as long?

Thomas Edison Invented Here
Southwest of Encampment

"What do fishing and lightbulbs have in common?" The question sounds like the beginning of a joke, but it's not. It's not even the beginning of a limerick or a riddle. Fishing and lightbulbs have nothing in common, but here at Battle Lake the former did quite possibly inspire the invention of the latter.

In 1878 Thomas Edison, supposedly needing a bit of a break from his laboratory in Menlo Park, New Jersey, came to Wyoming Territory for an astronomical-themed vacation. Edison rode the Union Pacific Railroad all the way out and disembarked in Rawlins, where several noted astronomers had gathered to watch a solar eclipse. Edison caught the eclipse—evidently from the doorway of a chicken coop, whose residents almost knocked him over in their biologically inspired haste to get back home after the sky went dark, but that's another story—and used it to test his tasimeter, an invention designed to detect and measure heat. (He wanted to see if the sun's corona had any heat of its own.) The work part of his vacation finished, Edison started off for a bit of sightseeing and outdoor activity. His sponsor, Henry Draper, a medical doctor, insisted that they go to Battle Lake because, even back then, its fish were of legendary size. It wasn't the fish, however, that ended up getting Edison's attention. His frayed bamboo fishing rod inspired a "Eureka!" moment that ultimately led to him inventing the first commercially practical incandescent lamp.

While sitting around a fire one night, perhaps trading tall tales of ones that had got away, Edison's rod tipped over and fell into the fire. Watching its frayed ends burn, Edison realized that the key to solving the lightbulb problem he had been working on for years might be to use nonconducting carbon filament. Upon returning to Menlo Park,

Edison set about testing this fishing-inspired idea. A year later, he successfully debuted the world's first incandescent lamp.

In case you're wondering, time has done little to diminish the reputation of Battle Lake's fish being extraordinarily large. If you happen to have a fishing rod (and a Wyoming state fishing license, of course) in hand when you go there to pay your respects to the lightbulb, Thomas Edison would approve. You'll find Battle Lake about 14 miles southwest of Encampment on Highway 70 (which is closed from October through May).

Always Cool
Jeffrey City

Travelers on the Oregon Trail didn't make their way west hauling freezers—the contraptions were bulky, and the first practical refrigeration machine had only been invented a few years prior in 1834. That made the ice waiting for pioneers here at Ice Slough, in the middle of the Wyoming desert, even more welcome. The fact that it wasn't some local entrepreneur selling ice to emigrants but rather a frosty treat courtesy of Mother Nature made it downright miraculous. And it was available nearly the entire summer.

At Ice Slough, water trickling anywhere from a few inches to a few feet beneath the peaty, sedge- and grass-covered surface would freeze solid in winter. Come spring and summer, even with above-ground temperatures soaring into the eighties and nineties, the sedges and grasses above would keep the water below sufficiently insulated that it stayed frozen. On the surface Ice Slough looks completely unremarkable, but parched, weary travelers could dig down just a short distance and come up with more ice than they had seen in months.

CENTRAL

Today, much of the water that once made the Ice Slough icy is drained off for irrigation. Still, some ice does manage to form during particularly wet years, although not so much that it can stay frozen through most of the summer. It's a good thing freezers are more portable and more popular these days. The Ice Slough is a bit less than 10 miles west of Jeffrey City on U.S. Highway 287.

Disappearing Right Before Your Eyes
Lander

A major river can't just vanish, can it? It can if you're at Sinks Canyon State Park looking at the Middle Fork of the Popo Agie (pronounced po-po-zsha). The Popo Agie (which means Tall Grass River in the Crow language) rushes out of Wyoming's largest mountain range, the Wind River Mountains, and into Sinks Canyon. It flows merrily along for quite some time until it suddenly turns into a large cave and, as the name of the park and canyon suggest, sinks underground. Not until ¼ mile later does the river reemerge at a large, calm pool, called the Rise.

For a long time no one was sure the water at the Rise was the same water that disappeared into the Sink, but then some scientist types did dye tests and proved the two were one and the same. Tests also revealed that more water emerges at the Rise than goes in at the Sink. And no one knows where the water goes for the two hours it takes to get from the Sink to the Rise. There are a few local theories, but we'll leave the pleasure of asking for directions to Lander-Atlantis and descriptions of giant sea monsters to you.

Better Hit It Just Right
Lander

No one wants to be laughed at. Especially by an antelope. And even more especially by a fake antelope on a plaque. Hunters failing to fell an antelope in the annual One Shot Antelope Hunt must suffer that indignity, however. While those participating hunters who do shoot and kill an antelope—and rules require that the killing must be done with only one bullet; if a hunter has to shoot a second time to kill the creature, it's considered a "miss"—get a plastic-encased silver bullet, those who come out of the field empty-handed (yet full of excuses) get a plaque with a laughing antelope on it.

Founded in 1940 by two hunting buddies marveling over the difficulty of hunting in pioneer days, when muzzle-loading rifles required the first shot to be deadly since its noise would cause all the prey to scatter, the One Shot Antelope Hunt has spawned imitator events elsewhere in North America and in Africa. Nonetheless, the original event in Lander remains the most popular one and has drawn celebrities such as Larry Hagman, Chuck Yeager, Roy Rogers, General Norman Schwarzkopf, and opera star Lauritz Melchior.

The One Shot Antelope Hunt is held annually in Lander on the opening day of the antelope-hunting season. The awards ceremony, where the losers get their laughing antelopes, is held the evening of hunt day and is open to the public. For more information call (307) 332–3356.

It's All in the Eye of the Beholder
Medicine Bow

There might not be too much competition in the "largest jade bar in the world" category, but even if it was a heated contest, the bar in Medicine Bow's Dip Bar would put up a good showing. Its 40-foot-long bar, installed in 1981, is all jade and all came from a single four-and-a-half-ton boulder. Depending on who's telling the story, the jade boulder was found in either Lander or Rock Springs.

The surprising thing about the world's largest jade bar is that it's not even the first thing you notice when you walk into the Dip. That would be all the painting. When Bill Bennett bought the Dip—a name derived from the *Diplodocus* dinosaur, fossils of which have been found nearby—in the mid-1980s, he hated the sunken dance floor. Bill hated it so much that it was the first thing he set about fixing. He had it raised to the level of the rest of the floor in no time. But Bill wanted to differentiate it somehow from the rest of the bar's floor, so he thought to paint it.

Initially, he planned on painting a likeness of his wife, but she objected on the grounds that she didn't want people walking on her all day long. Bill instead ended up going with western, wildlife, and ranch scenes, including scenery from the ranch he grew up on. The Dip's dance floor is the only handpainted dance floor west of the Mississippi. (Again, another category in which there might not be too much competition.)

Liking how the dance floor turned out, and still needing to put his wife's image somewhere, Bill kept on painting . . . and painting and painting. Mrs. Bennett ended up on the cafe ceiling. Bill covered everything else with more western-themed work. Nowadays, nearly everything in the bar, excluding the jade bar itself but including the cafe tables, is covered in paint. And you'd never guess that Bill is colorblind. The Dip is at 202 Lincoln Highway. For hours and other information call (307) 379–2312.

NOT EVEN CLOSE

Not only does Wyoming have fewer people than any other state in the country, but the few residents it does have are outnumbered by cattle. There are 2.8 cows for every person in Wyoming.

Real Demons or Dreamed Up?

Pedro Mountains

Sheb Wooley made Purple People Eaters famous in his song of that same name, but have you heard of Little People Eaters? Several Native American tribes who once lived in this area have legends telling of 20-inch-tall demons killing with miniature bows and poisoned arrows. Although no conclusive proof of any Purple People Eaters has surfaced, a mummy found here lends some credence to the idea that Little People Eaters aren't just the stuff legends or hit songs are made of.

In 1932 two men prospecting for gold here used dynamite to blast away a section of granite that was interfering with what they thought might be a particularly rich vein of gold. When the dust cleared, the men found something they definitely were not expecting: the skeleton of a man. Or of a sort-of man. He was sitting cross-legged on a ledge, nearly perfectly preserved, with brown wrinkled skin, heavy-lidded eyes, and thin lips. Cecil Main and Frank Carr could even see the man's fingernails. Seated, the man was only about 8 inches tall. Not that the miners tried to stretch him out, but they guessed that standing he would have been about 18 inches tall.

The duo took the little guy to Casper, the nearest city, and scientists came from all over to investigate, although most assumed the mummy was some sort of hoax. The find was intriguing enough to draw scientists from the American Museum of Natural History. Extensive tests were performed and X-rays taken. No signs of fraud could be discovered. In fact, the X-rays showed a perfectly formed, manlike skeleton. Just on a miniature scale.

The scientists who had come to disprove the find ended up deciding the mummy was a full-grown adult of an unknown Indian tribe, who had been approximately sixty-five at the time of his death. They were even able to tell that his spine was damaged, his head smashed in, and his collarbone broken. Based on these findings, the scientists surmised that the homunculus had died a violent death. All this poking and prodding and the test results were allegedly later certified by Harvard University's Anthropology Department.

Since certified mini-mummies were few and far between, this little man spent several years touring the country with carnival freak shows. A Casper businessman eventually purchased the remains and took them to New York City, where they were stolen just before his death. The remains have never resurfaced.

Even though the mummy disappeared, evidently his X-rays survived and were taken to a professor of anthropology at the University of Wyoming a few decades after the original examinations. This professor's findings weren't nearly as interesting as the first round's: He said he thought the skeleton was that of an infant suffering from some sort of congenital defect that caused unusual proportions in the bones, although he couldn't say which Indian tribe the infant might have been from.

The two prospectors who found the mummy went back to work, naming their mine the Little Man Mine. You can still find a sign in the Shirley Basin with the mine's name on it. Main and Carr never did find any gold here, though.

Baby Grand
Powder River

For those thinking about heading south to Arizona and the Grand Canyon, save time and money and hit Hell's Half Acre instead. But remember to bring your own water (more about that later). Sure, the Grand Canyon might be slightly bigger (by more than one million acres), but Hell's Half Acre—which is actually 320 acres—has *Starship Troopers*. The sci-fi flop was filmed here in 1996. It is a rich archaeological site as well: Everything from bison bones to rocks reddened by Native American campfires are just below the surface.

Despite the small difference in scale, Hell's Half Acre does rather resemble the Grand Canyon, with alien landscapes, a rainbow of rock and soil colors, and giant towers and spires caused by erosion. Hell's Half Acre could also use your tourism dollars a bit more. Even with all of these attractions, not to mention a big-budget Hollywood flick having been filmed right here, the visitor services have gone bust in recent years. There used to be a Hell's Half Acre cafe, gift shop, and motel, but the motel was just demolished, and the cafe and gift shop are now boarded up.

A lack of visitors is certainly partially to blame, but so is water. The water here might have been perfect for sculpting the rocks into fascinating forms, but it's not fine for drinking. The Hell's Half Acre water supply has more iron in it than even Popeye could stand. In 2004, the last year any services were open here, Natrona County had to truck in $30,000 of potable water from Casper, 44 miles away. Maybe it would just be cheaper to send everyone to the Grand Canyon. Hell's Half Acre is 5 miles west of Powder River on U.S. Highway 20/26.

He Grew Up to Be a Shoe
Rawlins

After dying in 1881, George Parrot did anything but rest in peace. The outlaw, more commonly known as Big Nose George for reasons that are obvious as soon as you see a photo, was skinned, tanned, and turned into a pair of shoes! And doorstop. And death mask.

In the late 1870s Big Nose George was running with a gang of horse thieves and robbers. In 1878 the group, which most likely also included Frank and Jesse James, decided to go big and rob a Union Pacific train. After they had meddled with the tracks, their plan was discovered, and a two-man posse was sent to track them down. The two deputies found the outlaws, who shot their pursuers.

Killing lawmen was a much more serious affair than attempted robbery, and the gang knew that a larger, and more determined, posse would now come looking for them; they split up, and everyone went their own way. Big Nose George managed to elude capture until 1880, when he drunkenly boasted about the attempted robbery and murders in a bar in Miles City, Montana. He was brought back to Rawlins for trial.

Big Nose pleaded guilty and was sentenced to be hanged in four months. But he had other ideas. Somehow filing through his shackles, Big Nose attacked jailer Robert Rankin, fracturing his skull and cutting his scalp. Hearing a commotion, Robert's wife, Rosa, came running and, thanks to the pistol in her hand, convinced Big Nose to return to his cell. Although the attempted escape was thwarted, Big Nose still ended up getting out of jail that evening—just not voluntarily. As word of the attempted escape spread throughout the city, a small group of citizens took justice into their own hands. They broke into the jail, kidnapped Big Nose, and hanged him from a telegraph pole near the corner of Front and Third Streets.

An undertaker prepared Big Nose for burial—there's a rumor his big nose required that the lid of the coffin be nailed in place to stay shut—but before he could be buried, John E. Osborne, a young doctor, had the casket opened and the body removed. Osborne wanted to study Big Nose's brain to see if there was any physical reason for his bad behavior. To get to Big Nose's brain, the good doctor crudely sawed off the top of the skull. This portion of the skull being unnecessary to Osborne's research, he gave it to his assistant, Lillian Heath (who went on to become Wyoming's first female doctor). Heath used the skullcap as a doorstop for years.

Finding no difference between Big Nose's "bad" brain and a "good" brain, Dr. Osborne moved on to other things. First, using plaster of paris, he molded a death mask of Big Nose. Osborne couldn't mold Big Nose's ears, however, as they were worn off during the lynching. Getting increasingly macabre, Osborne next removed the skin from the cadaver's thighs and chest. He sent the skin to a tannery in Denver with the instructions to make him a pair of shoes with it, specifically asking that the nipples be included. The rest of Big Nose was pickled in a whiskey barrel and eventually buried in the yard behind another doctor's office, not to be found until workmen were excavating in the area in 1950.

When Osborne got his new shoes, he was disappointed to see that the tannery had neglected to follow his instructions regarding including Big Nose's nipples. Even so, the two-toned lace-ups evidently were still among his favorite footwear. And evidently Wyomingites of the time didn't think that the good doctor was all that outlandish in his treatment of the dead. John E. Osborne was elected governor of Wyoming a little more than a decade after tanning Big Nose and wore Big Nose to his inauguration and inaugural ball. (From his position as governor,

Osborne went on to become a U.S. congressman, but there is no record as to whether he took Big Nose with him to Washington, D.C.)

You can see the remains of Big Nose George at the Carbon County Museum, at 904 Walnut. Call (307) 328–2740 for hours.

AHEAD OF HIS TIME

In 1884 blacksmith James Candlish took a break from his usual projects to build the first truly mobile home, right here in Rawlins. Candlish's all-in-one wagon, designed with sheepherders in mind, was so well configured—compact beds that can be stored away, plenty of storage space, tables that are folded down when not in use—that it is still used in sheep wagons made today. Even the modern-day equivalent of sheep wagons—RVs—are often modeled on Candlish's design. He came up with his design by combining elements he found in everything from military transport vehicles to ships. His first sheep wagon has gone on to greener pastures, but the Carbon County Museum has a fully kitted-out replica on display.

Seeing Red
Rawlins

If you think the rocks just north of town are a familiar shade of red, you're right. From the 1870s until the early 1900s, paint made from the hematite mined from these rocks colored everything from barns to the Brooklyn Bridge. "Rawlins red" was all the rage. Over a billion tons of ore were extracted during the mine's lifetime, and the paint made from it was shipped around the country. Although the 520-million-year-old Flathead Sandstone in which the hematite is found is still plentiful, the mine has been permanently closed for about a century. Advancements in the manufacturing of paint as well as the expense required to extract, process, and ship the ore made natural "Rawlins red" obsolete. Its legacy lives on, however; synthetically dyed paints are still available in the color.

Take a Breather
Rawlins

Five men were killed in the gas chamber at Wyoming's "Old Pen" during its eighty years housing the state's most notorious lawbreakers. Nowadays, you can enjoy the scare without the gas. The prison closed in 1981 . . . at least to prisoners. After cleaning it up—and unhooking the gas lines into the gas chamber—tourists were welcomed beginning in 1987. It's not unusual for an ex-inmate, one who escaped the gas chamber the first time around, to return as a visitor and want to sit in the hot seat. You'll find the Wyoming Frontier Prison Museum at 500 West Walnut Street; for more information call (307) 324–4422.

Wyoming's "Old Pen," where you can go and visit the gas chamber.

Just a Couple of Guys with a Mike and a Great Idea
Rawlins

Spending his high school years in Rawlins, Russ Leatherman didn't have to wait in long lines to get into a movie. The town's three movie screens were more than enough for its population of 11,000. After he moved to Los Angeles, however, Russ did have to stand in line at the movies. And one night, while standing in line, he and two friends came up with an idea that has revolutionized the way the entire nation goes to the movies. That idea was Moviefone, an easy-to-remember, interactive phone number that moviegoers could call to get all the showtimes and movie information they needed. No more searching through newspapers or calling every theater in town. Today, Moviefone and Movie fone.com are the most used movie guides in the country, helping millions of moviegoers weekly.

Russ isn't just one of the brains behind Moviefone, though. He is *Mr. Moviefone*. It's his voice that callers hear when they call Moviefone. It isn't that Russ was the most qualified for the announcer position when Moviefone launched; it's that he and his friends didn't have enough money to hire a professional voice actor even after they had all mortgaged their homes and maxed out their credit cards. Not having money to pay a professional, the three founders thought they'd give it a try themselves. They sat down in front of a microphone and recorder, and each practiced saying "press one, press two." One founder had a thick midwestern accent. Another sounded like Donald Duck. When it was Russ's turn, he said, "Hello and welcome to Moviefone!" in a "Dick Clark on crack" voice and was immediately declared to be Mr. Moviefone.

And Russ has been doing it ever since. His Mr. Moviefone voice has made it onto *The Simpsons, Saturday Night Live,* and *Late Show with David Letterman* and was even the subject of an entire episode of

Seinfeld. Even though Russ's idea has grown into a multimillion-dollar business and handles calls from nearly three million moviegoers per week, Rawlins and its three movie screens still aren't in Moviefone's service area.

Wyoming Gumbo
Red Desert

You might think Louisiana is the home of gumbo, but Wyoming is famous for it, too; Wyoming's version isn't nearly so tasty, though. In fact, Wyoming's gumbo is such that you hope to never encounter it. Mostly found in the Red Desert, gumbo is a deceptive dirt that in dry conditions is rock hard and with the addition of rain becomes the stickiest, slickest surface around.

Driving through the Red Desert, you'll first notice that you're in gumbo country when you see a sign along the lines of ROAD IMPASSABLE WHEN WET. You're not going to believe the dirt road you're on could become *that* bad if it rains, but trust me, it's more likely that Jovians will land at the Green River Intergalactic Spaceport than that a wheeled vehicle can drive a mile on a wet Red Desert road. And if your car gets stuck in gumbo, don't try walking. Gumbo may make the roads *slick* to the point of impassable, but it will *stick* to your feet like you can't believe. There's a potentially true story about a dude who got lost out here just before a rainstorm. His body was found a few days later . . . with a foot of mud stuck on the bottom of each shoe.

You're Not Hearing Things

Red Desert

Wyoming might be at least 1,000 miles from the nearest ocean, but we have plenty of sand. And our sand sings.

The Killpecker Dune field, in the Red Desert just north and east of Rock Springs, is the largest active dune field in North America . . . and one of only a handful of noise-making dune fields in the world. Marco Polo wrote about weird sand sounds he heard while traveling through the Gobi Desert, and Charles Darwin heard the sand in Chile. There is also a "barking" beach in Hawaii. Unfortunately, there are no documented instances of the early explorers of this region hearing the Red Desert sand sing, but there is no doubt it sounds off today.

There are several supernatural explanations for the noise—alternately described as singing, booming, roaring, and whistling—but science explains it thus: Subsurface stationary sand acts as a giant amplifier for surface sand grains as they slip down the face of a dune. Both the underlying and the surface sand must be very dry for sound production, and the grains have to be more rounded and polished than those of "normal," silent sand. Because the Killpecker Dunes are constantly moving and growing—stretching ever eastward for 55 miles—they have plenty of opportunities to do their thing. Or do their sing.

IT'S GOOD TO BE BAD

Since it is about 4.5 million acres, the Red Desert is understandably divided into subsections. Most sections fall within the jurisdiction of the Bureau of Land Management (BLM). The Jack Morrow Hills area, one of the most popular with recreationists within the desert, is named for a local nineteenth-century thief that the BLM has officially termed a "bad man." We wonder what the BLM would have named in Jack's honor had he been good.

Washing Back Time
Riverside

Just west of Riverside, a 2½-mile round-trip hike from the Blackhall Mountain Road trailhead, is one of the country's oldest spas . . . of a sort. Bowl-shaped natural rock formations fill with rainwater and snowmelt, making them perfect alfresco bathtubs. Native Americans used them to clean up after hunting, and their early presence here gave the "spa" its name: Indian Bathtubs.

Breed and They Shall Come
Saratoga

Fish and fish eggs would seem to be an odd export for a landlocked state like Wyoming, but, as you've probably realized by now, Wyoming is full of the unexpected. Right here in Saratoga, fish and fish eggs (no, not for caviar) are grown and sent to stock waters from the Great Lakes to Tennessee and Arkansas. The Saratoga National Fish Hatchery, established in 1911, produces and distributes close to six million fish eggs and 10,000 actual fish every year. Included in these numbers are five million Lewis Lake trout eggs that will—thanks to their formative days spent up at high altitude in clean, mountain air—undoubtedly grow into the stars of the you-should-have-seen-the-giant-one-that-got-away tales told up and down the shores of the Great Lakes.

These lake trout eggs might have been conceived in Wyoming, but they grow up to foil the fishermen of the Great Lakes.

The Saratoga hatchery isn't just for fish, though. There is also a toad-rearing room. Yup, you read that right. A room dedicated solely to the rearing of toads. Have room in your house for one of those? But Saratoga doesn't rear just any old toads. Its rearing room is restricted to the Wyoming toad, found only in southwestern Wyoming and considered the most endangered amphibian in North America. Wyoming toads born and raised in Saratoga are being used for reintroduction efforts.

To tour the toad room and the fish facility, head northeast on County Road 207 for 4 miles from downtown Saratoga. If you hit the hatchery between late September and early November, there's the added bonus of being able to watch fish spawn. I know, it sounds about as exciting as watching grass grow, but it's actually pretty cool. For more information call the hatchery at (307) 326–5662.

EARTHLY RICHES

Wyoming has more natural resources than almost any other state. Wyoming has 30 percent of the country's uranium-ore reserves; ranks fourth in coal reserves, fifth in crude oil reserves, and seventh in gas reserves; and is the only place in the world where "miracle mud," or pascalite, is found.

Try at Your Own Risk

Saratoga

Smallpox isn't really a big problem anymore, but if it does happen to come back, you might want to stay away from the miracle cure that Native Americans came up with. Area Native American tribes called present-day Saratoga "place of magic waters" and for years had come here to soak in its natural hot springs. When smallpox began to decimate their tribes, elders began advocating that infected tribe members sit in the spring's 118-degree waters and then jump into the nearby North Platte River, which was a much, much more temperate 40 degrees. Unfortunately, everyone who tried this miracle cure died.

With such decidedly negative feedback, you might think that would have been the end of people using these springs for health, but it wasn't. White men had to make their own mistake. This second attempt at healing through hot springs was more far-reaching, but thankfully the consequences were much less dire. In 1911 local entrepreneurs bottled the spring's water, labeled it as "radioactive mineral waters"—this is back when "radioactive" was actually believed to be a good thing—and distributed it nationally. While no one who purchased and drank the radioactive mineral waters died, the business didn't succeed.

In 1917 the state of Wyoming acquired the springs, directed the hot water into a poured-concrete pool, and opened it as a free public park. Engineers constructed a system that cools the water down a bit from the 118 degrees it is when it comes out of the ground. Hobo Pool hovers at close to a comfortable 105 degrees and is open daily. There are still plenty of people—and no medical research to refute this—who believe a soak a day keeps the doctor away. Hobo Pool is on Highway 30 in Saratoga.

If you're looking for more upscale hot springs, head to the Saratoga Hot Springs Resort, where you can have a tepee-covered minipool all to yourself and the main pool's walls aren't blanketed in algae and moss (like those at Hobo Pool).

Ich Habe Ein Milkshake
Shoshoni

Unless it's for one of the world's best shakes or malts, you can't get a prescription filled at Yellowstone Drug. The store, on the corner of Main Street and Highway 26 and once a mercantile shop owned by the grandfather of President Gerald Ford, has been an old-fashioned soda fountain recommended the world over—although not necessarily by doctors—for decades.

On a big day, milkshakes served outnumber local residents.

During summer months the store can be so busy that customers—sometimes speaking German, Russian, Japanese, or French—have to take numbers and wait outside to order their hand-mixed malt or shake. Owner Rachael Goff says she has gotten customers from Australia who ended up at Yellowstone Drug because neighbors back home recommended it. Once inside, customers choose from sixty-two flavors of hard ice cream, including the ordinary (vanilla, chocolate, praline) and odd (licorice, Mexicali mocha). Still can't find exactly what you want? Go ahead and combine any two flavors.

While Yellowstone Drug is busy throughout the summer and fall, it set a record on May 29, 2000, with 727 shakes in a single day. That's a shake every forty-four seconds.

Owners say the secret lies in the ice cream. More specifically, the secret is in the cream part of the ice cream. Yellowstone Drug only uses ice cream that has a very high percentage of butterfat. Now that's a prescription we're happy to take! Yellowstone Drug is at 127 Main Street. Call (307) 876–2539 for hours.

The sign says it all.

NOT YOUR MODEL INNKEEPER

The Four Seasons would definitely not approve of former South Pass City innkeeper Polly Bartlett. For that matter, Motel 6 probably wouldn't even hire her. Operating in South Pass City during its few short years as a mining boomtown (1867–1880), Bartlett supposedly laced her unsuspecting guests' meals with arsenic and, after they had made their way to the great inn in the sky, took their gold. A victim's relative finally caught onto Bartlett and, with the help of a gun, permanently relieved her of both her innkeeper's duties and her need for gold. Polly Bartlett was buried in an unmarked grave at the edge of town. Today, South Pass City is a ghost town and State Historic Site and said to be haunted by Bartlett's spirit.

A Joke Taken Too Far
South Pass City

You'd like to think that Wyoming was the first state to give women the right to vote because its early politicians were of a forward-thinking sort. And that may very well be the case. It may also very well be the case that William Bright, a South Pass City saloon and mine owner and representative to the first territorial legislature, authored and introduced a women's suffrage bill to appease his wife Julia, who evidently nagged him quite unmercifully over the issue . . . and because he knew it would never get passed. Evidently, it may also be that the bill made it through the territorial legislature because other representatives thought the same way: "We certainly don't want to look like cads, not to mention get endlessly harangued by our wives, for not letting women vote. It won't do any harm for us to pass this bill, as Governor Campbell will never sign it into law." (Or something along those lines.)

Well, Governor Campbell did sign the bill into law in December 1869, and Wyoming, whether it really wanted to or not, became the first territory or state to allow women to vote and hold public office. It was a South Pass City resident, Esther Hobart Morris, who shortly thereafter became the country's first woman judge when county commissioners appointed her justice of the peace. During her eight months in the post, she tried twenty-six cases.

A Different Sort of Slant
Superior

No, the builders of the Union Hall weren't intoxicated when they were putting the structure up in 1921. For whatever reason, the town wanted a trapezoidal meeting and social spot rather than a plain old rectangular one. So a trapezoid it was, and is . . . at least the exterior walls that remain standing today. This wasn't the only odd building in Superior, though. Home to 2,700 people during its heyday in the mid-1940s—it was one of the biggest coal-mining towns in the state—Superior once had row after row of homes made from train boxcars. They have long since disappeared, though, not even leaving walls behind as evidence of their uniqueness.

Trapezoidal Union Hall.

A River Doesn't Run Through It
Wamsutter

While there's a spot in the northwestern part of the state you can stand with one foot submerged in water flowing to the Atlantic and the other foot in water rushing to the Pacific, the Continental Divide goes out of its way—literally—to avoid much of the middle of the state.

An area the size of Rhode Island and Delaware combined, the Great Divide Basin is completely and totally shunned by the Continental Divide. At the top of the basin, the Continental Divide splits. One arm heads east and a bit south. The other heads west and a bit south. The two arms don't join again until more than 100 miles south from where they first split. The area directly south of that initial split, the Great Divide Basin, is left to its own devices to drain . . . which means that it doesn't drain at all. Rain or snow falling here has no choice but to sink into the soil or evaporate. Good thing it's in the middle of a desert and gets only 7 to 10 inches of precipitation a year—most of which is in the form of snow.

Despite its Rhode-Island-plus-Delaware-and-then-some size and being pretty much guaranteed to never be flooded, the Basin has fewer than 500 residents. Wamsutter is the only incorporated town.

A river doesn't run through it.

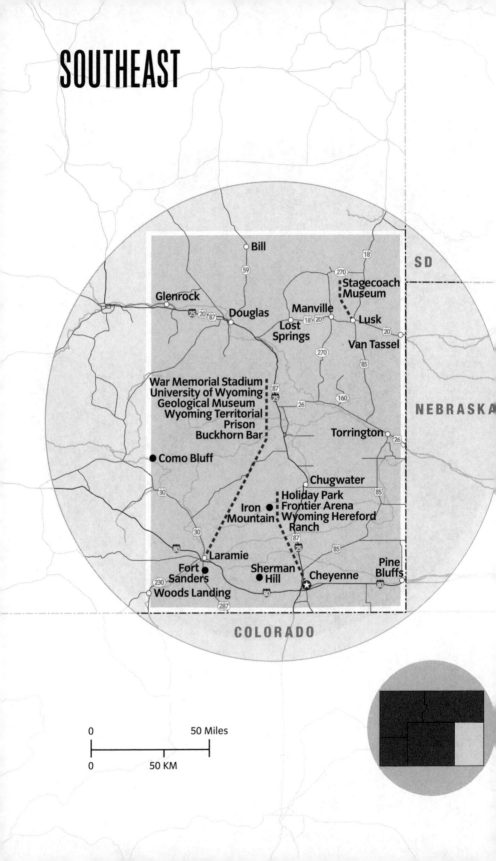

SOUTHEAST

Bill
59
18
SD
270
Stagecoach Museum
Glenrock
Manville
Douglas
25 20 87
18 20
Lost Springs
Lusk
20
270
Van Tassel
85
War Memorial Stadium
University of Wyoming
Geological Museum
Wyoming Territorial Prison
Buckhorn Bar
87
25
26
160
NEBRASKA
Torrington
26
Como Bluff
30
Chugwater
85
Holiday Park
Frontier Arena
Wyoming Hereford Ranch
30
Iron Mountain
80
87
25
85
Laramie
Pine Bluffs
Fort Sanders
Sherman Hill
Cheyenne
80
230
Woods Landing
80
287

COLORADO

0   50 Miles
0   50 KM

SOUTHEAST

This is one of the parts of Wyoming that give the state its undeserved reputation—one that I naively fell victim to believing—as a boring and empty wasteland. If you stick to Interstate 80 or Interstate 25, the only two roads in the entire state that have more than one lane traveling in each direction, you might fall prey to that same belief. Slow down, turn onto a back road, or wander about two of our largest cities, Laramie and Cheyenne, and "wasteland" will be replaced by "wondrous," "wild," and "weird"—the latter in only the best sense of the word, of course.

Pick up a copy of the only newspaper in the world named after a mule. Bust out a few new dance moves on the spring-loaded floor in Woods Landing. Attend a UW football game and enjoy being a part of the third-largest city in the state, even if this "city" is only in existence when the Cowboys play at home. Eat some of the 100,000 free pancakes that the Cheyenne Kiwanis, Boy Scouts, and Frontier Days volunteers griddle up over two days every July. When you're full, drive up to Lusk and the country's only memorial to the world's oldest profession. Read on for more southeastern adventures that are decidedly not boring.

No Water? No Problem!
Bill

Little Bill, Wyoming, might have the only yacht club in the world head-quartered in a general store. And Bill's is probably also the only yacht club that is both hundreds of miles from the nearest ocean and in the middle of a sage-strewn, high-altitude desert. For Bill (population between zero and three, depending on whom you talk to) to be any-where near water, you have to look back hundreds of millions of years—a minimum of 245 million—to the Paleozoic period. Back then, Bill, and the rest of Wyoming, was actually on the ocean floor. The Bill Yacht Club doesn't date back that far, though.

Looking for a way to make the Bill Store more profitable, David Munkres founded Bill Yacht Club in the mid- to late 1970s. Dean Munkres, David's father, had bought the Bill Store and its entire inven-tory for $12,500 in 1954 and later attained a degree of notoriety around the state for his "I've Been to Bill" bumper stickers. David started running the Bill Store (which back then did double duty as the Bill Post Office) in 1971, but each year business got slower and slower as more and more of the area's oil jobs disappeared. David thought that selling interesting T-shirts and hats could help his bottom line.

Today, David doesn't remember the inspiration behind the yacht club, but he does remember that right from the start he liked the name "Bill Yacht Club" for his hats and T-shirts. "It just came to me and I liked it," he says. "Simple." Not an artist himself, David described the new yacht club's logo to a printer, and the printer had an artist draw it up. The design—a boat surrounded by antelope and rabbits and anchored in sand—was an instant hit. Club "members" didn't seem to mind the yacht club's lack of basic facilities and water access.

David advertised in newspapers and magazines, and soon thousands of Bill Yacht Club hats and T-shirts were flying off the shelves and out through the mail to members across the country. He was selling these items well into the 1980s. David even got a call from a boater who had found a Bill Yacht Club hat floating in the middle of Lake Michigan.

Unfortunately, even with the yacht club's popularity—David estimates it received small write-ups in about 200 different publications—the store couldn't stay afloat, and David gave it up in 1988. However, the store's two subsequent owners have each kept the world's only desert-based boating group going. A few Bill Yacht Club T-shirts and hats with David's original design are still available at the Bill Store (307–358–6628). The yacht club's facilities remain as limited as ever, though.

One Whole Lot of Patience
Cheyenne

Some people collect stamps; other people ski. Cheyenne resident David Wimp counts. A retired army cook, David spends hours a day adding, or subtracting, depending on his mood, on a calculator; he has done so since 1982. He didn't even stop counting for his appearance on the Geraldo show. He calculated before the live audience and the millions watching at home on their televisions. As David told *Out West Newspaper*, "It's my hobby. I enjoy it."

Although David didn't begin counting with calculators until he was an adult, the beginnings of his hobby can be traced to high school, where a teacher promised him an "A" for writing down, in order, every number from one to one million. The teacher gave David nine days. Like most students, David was happy to do a bit of extra work for a high grade, and he quickly whipped out his pencil and started counting. Nine days later, however, David was only at 25,000. Obviously his enthusiasm for counting was not dampened by the failure.

The army didn't leave David too much time for counting, but soon after retiring from the military, he was at it again. David does his counting at a desk in front of his television. Proof of his counting competence—on February 26, 1989, David counted 7,070 numbers—lies in the miles and miles of homemade calculator tapes stored on bookcases in his home. Thinking white calculator tape too boring, David makes his own with colored construction paper. Laid end to end, the colorful tapes would easily stretch about 30 miles.

David usually adds, but after reaching two million for the first time, he did tire of the addition key. He subtracted back to zero, one number at a time. Now back to adding, David hopes to count to one billion. As a counter, he has probably already realized it will take more than one lifetime.

Once Guilty, Now Innocent, but Still Dead
Cheyenne

In 1903 a Cheyenne jury found gun-for-hire Tom Horn guilty of murder. It was a controversial trial, and in 1993 it was recreated, using all the same evidence and statements. This time around Horn was found innocent. It was ninety years too late, though; Horn had been hanged shortly after his trial concluded. The second trial was written up in the *New York Times* under the headline, "Once Guilty, Now Innocent, but Still Dead."

These days, even though it is generally agreed that Tom Horn didn't kill fourteen-year-old Willie Nickell, for whose murder Horn was hanged, the consensus is that he was rather overdue to hang for many other murders that he had undoubtedly committed. While working as an operative for the Pinkerton Detective Agency and later as a killer for hire for Wyoming and Colorado cattle barons, Horn killed between forty-two and forty-seven men. Seventeen of these killings were during shootouts. Out of all the famous lawmen/gunfighters of the Old West, only Bill Hickok has a more impressive shootout record.

During his time tracking down and killing cattle rustlers—which would have been from the late 1890s to the early 1900s, with a short break to serve in the army during the Spanish-American War—Horn received $600 for every rustler he permanently put out of business. Around that time, Horn is rumored to have said, "Killing men is my specialty. I look at it as a business proposition, and I think I have a corner on the market." Horn's trademark was to rest the head of his victim on a rock.

When Willie Nickell was shot on July 19, 1901, Horn was nearby. Horn's girlfriend lived around there, and it is thought that he was visiting her. Horn, however, wasn't arrested for the murder until 1903. That year, lawman Joe Lefors got—while Horn was drunk on alcohol Lefors had given him—a vague "confession" from the alleged murderer. During Horn's trial only parts of Horn's confession statement were used, completely changing the way it was comprehended. That wasn't the only fishy part of the trial, though. Two witnesses for the prosecution perjured themselves, and it was only the most circumstantial of evidence that placed Horn anywhere near the crime. But because of his profession, Horn was an easy target.

After Horn was found guilty and was waiting to be hanged, the local sheriff was so worried Horn might try to escape that he had armed troops surround the block where the jail and courthouse were located. A gunner was stationed in the jail every night. Horn didn't attempt to escape, though; he is said to have spent his time in jail weaving the rope he was hanged with.

Steamy Celebrity Wedding
Cheyenne

Most Hollywood couples spend a fortune to rent out entire islands or exclusive resorts where fancy friends and family can celebrate with them in style. Steve McQueen and Ali McGraw went for something a little different. Their wedding space was free, and they opted for steamy instead of stylish. The famous couple wed in Cheyenne's Holliday Park next to Union Pacific Big Boy 4004, one of the biggest and most powerful steam locomotives ever built. However, the couple was apparently more interested in Cheyenne itself than the 132-foot-long and 540-ton (with tender) behemoth Big Boy.

Big Boy 4004 might be the biggest—literally—wedding guest ever.

According to Cheyenne legend, Steve and Ali chose this wedding spot because they knew their nuptials would be written about in newspapers. Steve wanted the dateline to read "Cheyenne" rather than "Denver," their other Rocky Mountain–area option. "No one knows where Denver is, but, thanks to westerns, everyone in the world knows where Cheyenne is," he is rumored to have said.

Other couples have jumped on the bandwagon, or perhaps more appropriately, trainwagon. The Cheyenne Parks and Recreation Department reports that Big Boy is the guest of honor at a few weddings every summer. Interested? Just write a letter of intent to the park director, and he'll write back with a "yea" or a "nay." It's still free (although you do have to pay to rent out the park's sheltered picnic spaces).

Another famous Cheyenne train wedding: Ernest Hemingway and novelist and war reporter Martha Gellhorn married at Cheyenne's Union Depot in November 1940.

All Cracked Up
Cheyenne

Wyoming's replica Liberty Bell—awarded to the state in 1950 by the direction of the secretary of the treasury for the state's success in the U.S. Savings Bonds Independence Drive—rings with the same tone and has the same crack as does the original in Philadelphia. Thanks to differences in humidity between Philly and the mountain West, however, it has developed a few new cracks of its own. The bell, a 2,000-pound beauty cast in Annery-le-Vieux, France, exactly matches the dimensions of the original bell and supporting structure, but Wyoming's dry air has caused the wooden beam that suspends it to crack. It's a good thing this bell's traveling days are behind it: The bell was displayed in every part of the state between May and July 1950 but has enjoyed a permanent home on the southwest corner of the Capitol Building grounds ever since.

This isn't the only Liberty Bell Wyomingites have had the opportunity to see. In 1915, while on a cross-country train journey from Philly to the Panama-Pacific International Exposition in San Francisco, the original Liberty Bell—the same one that chimed out on July 8, 1776, for the first public reading of the Declaration of Independence—stopped at Cheyenne's Union Pacific depot for a few hours. People came from all over to see it.

Ninety-nine Bottles of Beer on the Wall
Cheyenne

There's a house 25 miles west of Cheyenne where the bottles are not only on the wall but actually are the wall. J. H. Widholm spent twelve years collecting bottles and designing a house he could make with them. But rather than use inconveniently shaped beer bottles (inconveniently shaped for construction, at least), Widholm went with formaldehyde bottles. Their rectangular shape stacked nicely, almost like bricks. There's also a rumor that Widholm was an undertaker and had easy access to as many formaldehyde bottles as he wanted. By the mid-1960s he had amassed more than 30,000 bottles and set about building his 54-by-20-foot house.

While the idea of a bottle house seems rather unique, Widholm doesn't claim credit for inventing the idea. He drew his inspiration from a similar structure he saw at Knott's Berry Farm amusement park in California. Widholm's is unique for the fact that it was built as a private home. Despite the house being all glass—the roof bottles are stacked horizontally lengthwise, and the walls have the bottle bottoms facing outward—he even included a few windows. There's also an inside fireplace.

Widholm no longer lives in the house, but its current residents care for it as much as he did. Vicki Launer grew up near the house and had always liked it. Several times, she and husband, Sonny, approached the former owners about buying it. The sale finally went through in 2003. Vicki says, "I grew up near the bottle house and was always fascinated by it. It looked like a fun place to live." The two use the bottle house as a cabin retreat from their everyday lives in Cheyenne.

Vicki and Sonny aren't the only ones who appreciate the uniqueness of their home these days. In November 2005 Home and Garden Television spent ten hours in and around the house, and it was featured in April 2006 on an episode of the network's *Offbeat America*. The segment attracted lots of interest to the house. Too much interest, in fact. The Launers are no longer publicizing where the house is located for fear someone might vandalize it. After all, it doesn't take much to hurt a glass house.

GIVING THE FINGER

Because Wyoming is generally rural and has few interstates, most passing motorists wave to each other. But, before you start flapping your wrist, know this: The Wyoming Wave doesn't involve the full hand. When you see a car approaching from the other direction, merely raise your first finger off the steering wheel—not the middle one as people often do in big cities—and there you are. On dirt or gravel roads, a nod of the head is acceptable.

Neil Diamond Slept Here
Cheyenne

Neil Diamond might be famous for "Kentucky Woman," among other songs, but he himself was a Cheyenne Boy. The sequin-clad crooner lived in Cheyenne for a few years during elementary school. He has been quoted as saying, "I was very young, but it was a great experience; very different from Brooklyn. Cheyenne was just chock full of cowboys and great stuff that you only see on films." The Diamond family found themselves in Cheyenne because father Keive, who was in the army, was temporarily stationed at the F. E. Warren base. The Diamonds were in Cheyenne for only a few years and then moved back to Brooklyn, where Neil was given his first guitar at age sixteen and signed a contract with Sony Records three years later. He had a fencing scholarship to New York University, but Diamond dropped out just before graduation to devote all his time to songwriting. The rest is history, "If You Know What I Mean." The rumor is that he still makes an annual trip back to Cheyenne around New Year's.

Yellow Page
Cheyenne

There weren't many places for your fingers to do the walking when the Wyoming Telephone and Telegraph Company published the first phone book with advertising in the country in 1881. The first-ever Yellow Pages—which today can weigh more than ten pounds in larger metro areas—was but a single page. It was definitely yellow, though. The printer hired by the phone company didn't think he had enough white paper to print the necessary number of copies, and, not wanting to have half printed on white and the other half on a different color, he abandoned white entirely for a color of paper he had plenty of. The advertising/business sections of phone books have been printed on yellow paper ever since.

That single, yellow page had most everything the technologically savvy of the time needed to know. It listed each and every of the 102 Cheyenne residents and businesses with phones as well as what made this phone "book" so revolutionary: six ads. The ads were for confections, ice cream, dry goods, groceries, jewelry, and boots. Even though the book has grown exponentially in size, some things about it haven't changed: The two boot companies advertising in 1881 both professed to have the lowest prices in town.

The page also managed to save room for instructions for phone users:

1. Report promptly to this Office any irregularity in the working of your instrument. Such reports should be made in writing, and addressed to the Manager.
2. Telephone Operators are expected to be courteous and obliging over the wires of this Company. Any violation of this regulation should be promptly reported to this Office by the Subscriber.
3. Subscribers will not only insure good service, but greatly oblige the Management, by reporting any and all irregularities (in the Central Office) that may come under their observation.
4. Subscribers to this Exchange will not allow persons who are not subscribers to use their instruments, without permission of the Company.
5. In case of Fire, please notify Central Office.

To Signal Central Office—Turn the Crank half around, and when through talking, give another half Turn.

USING WHAT YOU GOT

The first telephones in Wyoming used something the state already had plenty of: barbed wire. Telephone subscribers had barbed wire running from fences into their houses.

Pancakes for 'Em All!

Cheyenne

Cheyenne's annual Frontier Days Rodeo—the "daddy of 'em all"—brings hundreds of professional rodeo cowboys and hundreds of thousands of spectators to Cheyenne for ten days in July. Some of the best bronc bucking, steer roping, bareback racing, and bull riding you'll ever see happens here.

Now, not to steal any thunder from the rodeo cowboys, but their feats do rather pale in comparison to those of the Frontier Days staff, the city of Cheyenne, the local Kiwanis, and the Cheyenne Boy Scouts. Together, these volunteers turn 20,000 pounds' worth of ingredients into free pancake breakfasts for 30,600 (give or take a few hundred) hungry people. The tradition started in 1952 and has been going on, and growing, ever since. That first year, volunteers using World War I–era griddles fed pancakes to 1,000 people plopped down on bales of hay. (Not enough regular chairs could be rounded up.) By 1962 there were 1,500 people queuing up for flapjacks. Today, with tens of thousands lining up, the Kiwanis use the event as an emergency response training. The Frontier Days crowds simulate the hordes the Kiwanis might have to feed if some sort of natural disaster ever strikes the area. Boy Scouts help out for a custom-made Pancake Patch.

To make the 100,000 pancakes scarfed down by starving spectators, the volunteers use:

5,000 pounds of pancake mix
650 pounds of butter
450 gallons of syrup
4,000 pounds of ham
8,000 pounds of milk
12 gallons of cooking oil

Five hundred and twenty gallons of coffee, sweetened by 125 pounds of sugar, wash all those pancakes down. While the Kiwanis chefs are stretched out in a long line griddling up the cakes, the Boy Scouts run along behind them, catching flapjacks as they're flipped, over the griddlers' heads, from the griddle.

Feel like eating 100,000 pancakes?

A Not-So-Peaceful Final Resting Place
Cheyenne

There's a grave in Cheyenne that hundreds of thousands of people line up to visit each year. All right, so perhaps the people are not lining up for the grave itself, but rather for the event that's held on top of the grave. Ignore this little detail, though, and Steamboat the bucking bronc's popularity in death is somewhere in between that of President Coolidge and Elvis (much closer to Elvis than Coolidge).

The most famous, orneriest, meanest, buckingist bucking bronc in the world from 1901 until 1914, when he got blood poisoning from a wire cut and was shot, Steamboat was buried by the Frontier Arena grandstands. (He was actually shot right there and rolled into a just-dug grave.) Frontier Arena is the site of Cheyenne's annual Frontier Days, which is what the hordes actually line up for, and where Steamboat unseated more cowboys than any other horse.

Born on a ranch between Laramie and Bosler, Steamboat was named by cowboys who thought his snort sounded more like a steamboat whistle than a horse. He was owned by C. B. "Charlie" Irwin, a rancher, founder of Frontier Days, movie producer, racehorse breeder, champion steer roper, and friend of Teddy Roosevelt, Will Rogers, and even outlaw Tom Horn.

Even though Steamboat was known as the "horse that couldn't be ridden," a few cowboys did manage to stay mounted. Only a very few, though. Today's rodeos require cowboys to stay atop their animals for eight mere (long?) seconds, but back when Steamboat was bucking, cowboys had to stay on until the bucking stopped. The three cowboys who successfully rode Steamboat were in the saddle for hours! It wasn't unusual for a rider to last a few minutes on Steamboat and then, with muscles sore and tired, intentionally get himself tossed off.

Steamboat—whose trademark whistle came from a nose bone that was broken while he was being castrated—was inducted into the Pro-

Rodeo Hall of Fame in 1979. Being inducted into the Hall of Fame and having the most visited grave—kind of—in the state of Wyoming aren't Steamboat's only claims to fame, though. Notice the bucking-bronc logo on all University of Wyoming apparel? Well, that bucking bronc is Steamboat. In the early 1920s UW equipment manager Deane Hunton stumbled upon a photo of cowboy Gus Holt riding Steamboat. Hunton traced the photo and had it made into a logo. It's been the UW logo ever since.

Another note on the importance of bucking broncs in Wyoming: While the UW logo and the bronc and cowboy on Wyoming's license plates are similar, they are not the same horse or rider. The license-plate horse is Deadman, and his rider is most likely Albert Jerome "Stub" Farlow of Lander. Deadman did his bucking up in Jackson Hole and first appeared on the Wyoming license plate in 1936.

And one more horse tale: One horse came close to Steamboat's level of meanness. In 1930 rodeo contestants petitioned Frontier Days for the removal of the bronc Midnight from the finals, saying it wouldn't be fair to the cowboy who drew him. The rodeo board refused, wanting "to bar neither man nor horse." Midnight wasn't always tough, though. After tossing the unfortunate cowboy who drew him, Midnight would trot over to his owner's wife and eat sugar cubes out of her hand. In 1936 Midnight was buried next to his owner's other prize bronc. His tombstone reads:

> Under this sod
>   lies a great bucking hoss;
> There never lived
>   A cowboy he couldn't toss.
> His name was Midnight,
>   His coat as black as coal,
> If there is a hoss-heaven,
>   Please God, rest his soul.

Costly Cows

East of Cheyenne

A visit to the Wyoming Hereford Ranch (WHR) is like a visit to the homes of Brad Pitt and Ashton Kutcher . . . except this ranch's studs lived in barns and open fields. Utter the names "Prince Domino" or "Lerch" to anyone involved in the livestock business, and you'll get knowing nods. Mention that some of your cattle share the genes of these two champion bulls, and you'll get appreciative stares. Although both are now long gone, Prince Domino and Lerch helped make the Hereford breed one of the most prized among cattle. Both called the Wyoming Hereford Ranch home.

Still a sizable ranch—although asking a rancher the size of his spread is about as uncouth as asking how much money someone makes—the WHR was once even larger. When founded in 1873, the Swan Land and Cattle Company was one of the largest cattle outfits in the country. Its 113,000 head of cattle roamed over one million acres from Rawlins to Ogallala and from Cheyenne north to the North Platte River. The WHR was once a part of this behemoth. It was made its own division in 1882 with the arrival of the first Hereford, a cattle breed prized in beef production for its traits of early maturity and fattening ability. The next year, 146 Herefords arrived at the ranch from England. By the early 1900s WHR bulls were becoming known for their superior genetics. Starting after World War I, WHR bulls won twenty out of twenty-nine years at the National Western Carlot Hereford Bull Competitions. For those unfamiliar with cattle competitions, this one is the equivalent of the Super Bowl.

Today, Steve and Cathy Anderson manage the ranch, and the ranch's bulls are still known as among the best of the Hereford breed. While none have quite the shining star of Prince Domino or Lerch, there are a few famous-in-the-industry bulls loping about the ranch's fields. Visitors are more than welcome at the ranch, but the bulls don't give autographs. The Wyoming Hereford Ranch is 1 mile down Camp Stool Road, exit 367 from I–80. The ranch is on the right. For more information call (307) 634–1905.

Into Thin Air
West of Cheyenne

Nepal and China have Everest. Europe has the Matterhorn. Alaska has Mount McKinley. I–80 has Sherman Hill, between Cheyenne and Laramie. You could suffer and sweat yourself up to some aerie, but why do that when you can reach a huge summit without suffering or sweating and in the relative comfort of your car, perhaps even listening to satellite radio and munching on chips?

Abe Lincoln never made it here, but his giant head did.

At 8,640 feet above sea level, Sherman Hill is the highest point of all of I–80's 2,902.51 miles. But even though Sherman Hill is more than three times higher than I–80's highest point east of the Mississippi, near milepost 111 in Pennsylvania (that's only 2,550 feet), that lesser summit feels higher because you see your car climbing up it. The ascent up to Sherman Hill's heights is so long and gradual (coming from the east, it begins in Chicago; from the west, it begins in San Francisco) that most people don't even know they're climbing. That doesn't lessen the achievement, though; how about treating the car to some premium at the next gas station? It's been working hard!

Sherman Hill has another advantage over all those harder-to-reach high points listed above. None other than Abraham Lincoln is waiting to greet you at the Summit Rest Area. Or at least Abraham Lincoln's head—all 12½ feet of it. Moved here from the high point of the old Lincoln Highway when I-80 was built, this statue is the world's largest bronze head and weighs three and a half tons. Artist Dr. Robert Russin, a professor at the University of Wyoming, sculpted sixty-three separate pieces, bolted and welded them together, and then chased the seams to remove any signs of joints.

RECORD-SETTING ROAD

Experience a national record while driving the 77 miles along I–80 between Laramie and Walcott Junction. When it opened in October 1970, it was the longest single stretch of interstate highway ever opened at one time. It continues to hold the record.

WANDERING WATER

The layers of claystone, sandstone, and conglomerate rock around Chugwater collect rainfall and snowmelt that eventually end up in the country's breadbasket. The melted snow and rain soak into the rock here and seep east along the rock formation. All the wandering water eventually collects in a major groundwater aquifer beneath the Great Plains.

Antique Abode
Como Bluff

Even though the first permanent human-made structures didn't start dotting Wyoming's landscape until the nineteenth century, it is a Wyoming cabin built several decades after the territory was first settled that undisputedly claims the title of "The World's Oldest Building."

Astute minds with even the slightest mathematical bent might realize that the Egyptian pyramids, Mayan temples, Parthenon, Colosseum, and even the Empire State Building all predate (some by thousands of years) 1933, the year Wyoming's little cabin was built. So how can our little cabin be the world's oldest building? Well, being quite literal folk, Wyomingites say "world's oldest" because Fossil Cabin near Como Bluff is made entirely from dinosaur fossils that are between 100 and 200 million years old (average age: 145 million years). You can't get much older than that.

Discovered by Union Pacific Railroad workers in the 1870s, the Como Bluff dig site was first excavated in 1878. It was, and remains, one of the world's most renowned dinosaur fossil sites. Dinosaur fossils were so abundant that surveyors used longer ones as stakes! The remains of dozens of different dinosaurs were found here, including the giant *Diplodocus*.

Until recently, the *Diplodocus* was the largest animal ever unearthed. Today, a Como Bluff *Diplodocus* skeleton—72 feet long, 22 feet high, and estimated to weigh between fifty and seventy tons—stands in the New York Museum of Natural History. Another *Diplodocus* skeleton, this one 84 feet long, was discovered here in 1897 and was purchased by Andrew Carnegie for his Carnegie Museum of Natural History in Pittsburgh. The creature was named *Diplodocus carnegii*.

Andrew Carnegie liked his Dip so much that he had a full-size cast made in 1905 and personally presented it to King Edward VII for the British Museum. This triggered requests from other European royals and presidents. Casts were eventually installed in the capital cities of

There's no doubt this is the oldest building in the world.

Germany, France, Austria, and Italy and, a few years later, also in Russia, Spain, Argentina, and Mexico. Most of these casts are still on display. A fully fleshed-out cast of this *Diplodocus* was unveiled at Pittsburgh's Carnegie Museum of Natural History to celebrate the one hundredth anniversary of the fossil's finding. In all, Como Bluff excavations resulted in the discovery of twenty-six new species of dinosaur as well as forty-five new species of Jurassic mammals.

By 1933 most of the excavating was done, and a local entrepreneur, Thomas Boylan, hauled leftover fragments of dinosaur bone from the dig site. Using 5,776 bones that weighed a total of 102,000 pounds, he constructed a building that was to be used as a museum. Next door to the museum he erected another building, this time out of more traditional materials like stone, of roughly the same dimensions as a *Diplodocus*. To give museum visitors a notion of *Diplodocus*'s size, Boylan would point to the house next door and explain that many of the fossils pulled from Como Bluff, and used to make the museum, belonged to a creature every bit as wide and tall as that house.

A TRIP TO REMEMBER

Elementary-school kids on a field trip to Alcova Lake got more than they expected when they found a dinosaur skull and bones.

About 8 miles east of Medicine Bow on U.S. Highway 30, the Como Bluff Fossil Cabin Museum is open to the public throughout the summer. For those who really want to own a piece of history, at the time of this writing, the cabin and surrounding land were for sale.

WYOMING'S SECOND-OLDEST BUILDING

Leaving aside structures made from fossils, Wyoming's oldest building is "Old Bedlam." Built in 1849—using traditional building materials—by the army as a bachelor officers' quarters, the building supposedly earned its nickname from the activities of the young officers living there. It stands at the Fort Laramie National Historic Site, 3 miles up Highway 160 from the Town of Fort Laramie (which is at exit 92 from I–80).

Jackalopes Live Here
Douglas

You might think jackalopes, the endemic-to-the-West cross between a jackrabbit and an antelope, are about as real as the similarly elusive unicorn, but one visit to Douglas might just change your mind. The "Jackalope Capital of the World" celebrates this mysterious mammal with Jackalope Days on the second Friday and Saturday of every June; no fewer than four jackalope statues around town, ranging in size from 7 to 13 feet; and even an annual jackalope hunt from midnight to 2:00 A.M. on June 31. You can get your jackalope hunting license at the Douglas Area Chamber of Commerce.

Real or imaginary, jackalopes call Douglas home.

Although jackalopes are among the most hard-to-spot animals in life, there is no shortage of mounted jackalopes around Douglas. In fact, it was a Douglas taxidermist who, back in the 1930s, first thought to create, umm, stuff a jackalope. Douglas Herrick went out hunting jackrabbits with his brother Ralph. After the two returned home with their catch, Douglas tossed one of the dead jackrabbits onto the floor of his taxidermy shop. The jackrabbit happened to land next to a pair of mule deer horns. Douglas, who had learned taxidermy through a mail-order course, was hit by a bolt of inspiration.

Douglas's new crossbreed was an instant hit. Local Roy Ball bought it for $10 and put it on display in the town's Labonte Hotel, where it remained until thieves filched it in 1977. With their initial effort so successful, Douglas and Ralph made more and more mounted jackalopes. More interested in spreading fun than in making money, Douglas never patented his creation. By the late 1930s other taxidermists were stuffing their own jackalopes, and the creatures were featured on postcards and in magazine articles and even in movies and books. Even President Ronald Reagan was smitten with jackalopes. He had a mounted one hanging on a wall at his California ranch. When touring the property with reporters in the 1980s, the president joked—not that the reporters knew he was joking—that he had shot and killed the animal himself.

The jackalope market continues to expand today: If you can't catch a jackalope during the short Douglas hunting season, you can still buy jackalope milk. Thanks to the animal's powerful leaps, it comes already homogenized. Be careful with it, though—it is rumored to be an aphrodisiac.

If you are one of the fortunate few to come upon a jackalope in the wild, beware; their horns aren't just for show. Also called the "warrior rabbit," jackalopes are an aggressive species, although there have been no documented jack attacks. They are known to be wily when hunted. According to reports from hunters, jackalopes can mimic human sounds. To elude capture, they have been known to call out, "There he goes! Over there!" Jackalopes are known to be singers as well. A few cowboys have reported jackalopes singing back as the cowpokes sat singing around a campfire at night. These cowboys did not report how much, and what, they had been drinking when hearing such song.

Jackalopes aren't completely a creation of Douglas Herrick, though. There have been plenty of substantiated sightings of horned rabbits in the wild, some even predating the 1930s. Most likely these sightings are of regular rabbits infected with the Shope papillomavirus, which causes the growth of horn- and antlerlike tumors in various places on the rabbit's head and body. But don't let science spoil your fun.

MORE FUNNY RABBITS

Fifty-seven million years ago, Wyoming had rabbitlike creatures hopping about that would make jackalopes look run-of-the-mill. And while some people debate the existence of jackalopes, often putting them in the same category as unicorns and chimeras, there is no doubt that uintatheres really walked, or bounded, about the state.

Uintatheres are giant—about the size of a small elephant—horned rabbits. Seriously. In the early 1990s paleontologists unearthed uintathere fossils at an excavation site near Bitter Creek. These now-extinct creatures are thought to be cousins of today's rabbits. Or could it be that jackalopes are their more direct descendants?

Not Your Average Cow Horse

Douglas

Not that Sir Barton's pasture mates at J. R. "Doc" Hylton's ranch outside of Douglas knew, but they had the privilege to share grass with greatness of a type never found before or since in Wyoming. Sir Barton was the first ever winner of Thoroughbred racing's Triple Crown.

In 1919 Sir Barton won the Kentucky Derby, Preakness, and Belmont Stakes. He was so far ahead of his time, in fact, that the term "Triple Crown" hadn't yet been applied to this feat. Sir Barton's Triple Crown showing wasn't bad for a horse who lost six out of six races the year before and whose job in the Derby, the first of the Triple Crown races, was to act as a rabbit for his better-thought-of stablemate, Billy Kelly. Sir Barton went out fast at the beginning, led the entire race, and finished 5 lengths ahead of the second-place horse (which was Billy Kelly).

Sir Barton, despite such fickle feet as to require his farrier to line his shoes with piano felt, had one more good racing season in him before he was put to stud. His retirement was anything but easy, though. His owner went bankrupt, and Sir Barton found himself deeper in Middle America than perhaps any Thoroughbred champion had ever lived. Sir Barton had been sold to the U.S. Army Remount Service in Fort Robinson, Nebraska. His fate led him still farther into cowboy country. Doc Hylton, one of the few in this area who knew of Sir Barton's previous life, found him and brought him to his ranch outside Douglas. Sir Barton was back on stud duty, doing his best to improve the bloodlines of Doc's horses.

There is no evidence to suggest that Sir Barton did anything but enjoy his time siring foals under the Wyoming sun. He died of colic in 1937 and was buried at the ranch. In 1968, however, a Douglas horse fancier as well as the town's Jaycees decided that Sir Barton, despite being a racer rather than a rodeo star, deserved a monumental gravesite. He was exhumed and moved to the town's Washington Park, where a stone tablet, bronze plaque, and fiberglass statue honor him to this day.

You're Fired! Or Maybe Not

Fort Sanders

It was 1868, and one of the biggest showdowns in the West was about to happen, yet there wasn't a single cowboy, outlaw, or Indian around. Heck, there weren't even any face-offs on Main Street or guns drawn. Some firing was threatened, although not the kind of firing most commonly associated with the Wild West.

Let's back up a bit, though. Those at the front of the showdown were the Civil War's top brass from the Union army. Generals Ulysses S. Grant (who was about to win the presidency), William Tecumseh Sherman, Edward Potter, and John Gibbon were gathered in a room at Fort Sanders. It was the greatest-ever concentration of the generals who had won the war in the West. But why were they here? Was Wyoming Territory threatening secession? Did Wyoming have a slave trade going on?

We're happy to report that it was neither of those reasons that brought the generals west. Rather, a good friend and former coworker of theirs, General Grenville M. Dodge, was about to be fired from his position as head engineer with the Union Pacific Railroad. General Dodge was extremely good at his job, but the UP's vice president, a not-so-honest man who regularly directed railroad contracts to his own company, was worried that Dodge had too much power and could interfere with his profits. The Civil War generals weren't going to let their friend go down in flames. Talk about job security!

When the UP's vice president walked into the meeting with General Dodge, called specifically so he could fire Dodge, he was surprised. Not only was Dodge, calm as can be, waiting for him, but so were Dodge's friends Grant, Sherman, Potter, and Gibbon. Needless to say, it was immediately apparent that Dodge was the one with the power. The subject of firing wasn't even brought up at all.

The bit that remains of Fort Sanders—the ruins of an old stone guardhouse—is ¼ mile west of U.S. Highway 287 on Kiowa Street, 2 miles south of Laramie.

Just Doing His Job
Glenrock

Dee Zimmerschied was just doing his job, bulldozing away at an oil pad site north of Glenrock when he noticed he was scraping more than dirt. A weekend arrowhead hunter, Zimmerschied thought he might have found some old bones. Some pretty big, pretty old bones. In Wyoming when bones are unearthed, the law doesn't require that they be reported, but Zimmerschied, intrigued and thinking it might be something important, did tell his bosses. A week later professionals went out to examine the find.

Zimmerschied had been right. The bones were both big and old, having belonged to a woolly mammoth that had died no more recently than 12,000 years ago. Paleontologists from the Tate Museum at Casper College spent five weeks working the site, extracting about 300 bones and bone fragments. They think that once the pieces are put together, Zimmerschied's mammoth will be the largest one yet found in the state. Not bad for a day's work. When finished, the mammoth will live at the Tate Museum in Casper.

Columns of Casualties

Granite Cañon

No doubt the fancy-pants art critics in New York or London would have quite a bit to say about artist Pete Barajas's front yard off I–80 between Cheyenne and Laramie. The way Pete looks at it, though, he was just using stuff he had on hand to compensate for a lack of time on his part. Pete had always liked totem poles but never had the time to carve one himself. So instead of carving, he screwed. Pete screwed animal skulls, bones, and antlers collected during his years of hunting onto giant logs collected during his years of firewood gathering. It was quick. It was easy. It satisfied his desire to have a totem pole.

Wyoming artwork at its finest.

The first "Totem of Death" was started eight years ago. Pete, who usually applies his artistic talents to designing T-shirts and doing custom bikes and cars, has now completed three of these creations. (A few dead animal parts are tacked up elsewhere on the property as well.) Pete hasn't been counting the skulls, bones, and antlers he's put up, but they must total about one hundred. After all, the totems are each 14 feet tall. Equally intriguing as the totems—and just as open to artistic interpretation—is the cow skeleton nailed up onto the exterior wall of Pete's Harley shop. Pete took an entire skeleton and arranged it exactly as it was in life.

Pete does have a more traditional—that is, carved—totem to add to his collection, but he says he needs a crane to put it up since it is so big and heavy. Another score for the Totems of Death: They don't require anything more than one man, a drill, and some screws to assemble. Even if Pete wasn't trying to make any sort of statement with his totems, we'd still like to hear what an art critic has to say.

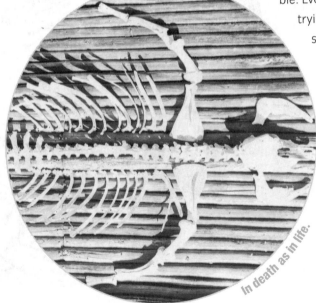

In death as in life.

Tiffany, Schmiffany

Iron Mountain

If you see something shiny on the ground when walking around Iron Mountain, pick it up. In the middle of what may be one of the most diamondiferous areas in the world, you could just get lucky. More than 100,000 gem- and industrial-quality diamonds have been found in Wyoming, and geology experts say that could be just the tip of the iceberg. Only a few miles on the wrong side of the Wyoming-Colorado border is the United States' first and only successful diamond-producing lode. Tens of thousands of stones, including a seventeen-carat monster whose starting bid at auction was $300,000, have been unearthed there. Besides Wyoming and Colorado, the only other state in which diamonds have been found is Arkansas.

But what's exciting about Wyoming's diamonds aren't the stones that have already been found, but the possibility of future finds. Only two known rock types are currently being mined for diamonds in the world, and Wyoming has lots of one of them, kimberlite. Hundreds of millions of years ago, kimberlite blasted up from 100 miles below the earth's surface. Traveling upward, which it did at twice the speed of sound, kimberlite sometimes exploded through layers of crystallized carbon (diamonds). And sometimes, the kimberlite would bring these diamonds all the way to the surface with it.

There are only 4,000 known kimberlite pipes in the world, making it one of the rarest rock types on the planet. Wyoming has more than a hundred of them. Historically, most have been concentrated near the Wyoming-Colorado border, but, since 1998, state geologists have identified approximately 80 percent more kimberlite deposits in the Iron Mountain area than were previously thought to exist. Iron Mountain is now recognized as one of the two largest kimberlite districts in the country.

Since word of Wyoming's diamondiferousness has gotten out, more than a few people have thought they had struck it rich. In the 1990s an entire family walked into the office of a senior state geologist with what they claimed to be the biggest diamond in the world. (A jeweler had told them so.) The state geologist immediately recognized it as nothing but a piece of quartz. To prove it to the family, he took out a tool and easily scratched the stone. The family was quite displeased their diamond had been marred and didn't listen when told that if their stone was in fact a diamond it wouldn't have gotten scratched. They demanded another geologist's opinion. The second geologist accidentally dropped the stone on the tile floor, and the giant "diamond" shattered into little pieces.

Want to go diamond hunting yourself? Kimberlite pipes are fairly easy to recognize. Trees don't grow on kimberlite, but grass grows slightly taller than usual. Because kimberlite is softer than the surrounding terrain, animals dig more burrows in it. The soil thus exposed is gray and rich in clay and is known as "blue ground." Who wants to be a rhinestone cowboy when you can be a diamond dude?

Rare Air
Laramie

College athletic departments will do anything to be competitive these days. Just look at the University of Wyoming. At 7,163 feet above sea level, its Laramie campus is the highest Division I school in the country. This means that athletes competing in Laramie must breathe the thinnest, least-oxygen-rich air of any school in the country.

All right, so maybe the school's founding fathers weren't thinking ahead to Wyoming–Colorado State football games back in 1887, when the school was established, but the rare air certainly works to the

Cowboys' advantage today. Most of the schools in the UW's Mountain West Conference come to Laramie from between 2,000 and 5,000 feet above sea level, although poor San Diego State comes to Laramie from sea level. There's a rumor that San Diego State once resorted to bringing bottled oxygen to Laramie and, when that didn't work, showing up for basketball and football games days in advance. The showing-up-early-to-acclimatize scheme didn't combat the effects of Laramie's altitude either—they still lost—so San Diego State then tried a totally different tack: arriving in Laramie at the last minute. The theory behind this was that the altitude wouldn't have time to affect the athletes.

Stats will show that none of these tactics helped San Diego State: In basketball Wyoming is 21–5 at home against San Diego State; in football the record is slightly closer, but the Aztecs have still lost to the Cowboys in Laramie twice as often as they win. The ironic thing is that even when the Cowboys travel to San Diego to play the Aztecs on their home turf, they still enjoy an advantage from living and training at elevation. Evidently, when your body is used to oxygen-rich sea-level air and you're competing against teams whose bodies like the thin stuff, you really can't win.

This city is only around when the Cowboys play home.

TEMPORARY TOWNS

When UW's War Memorial Stadium is filled, it is the third-largest city in the state (behind Cheyenne and Casper). When the Double A basketball arena is at capacity, it is the state's fifth-largest city.

The university's residence hall area has the state's highest population density, with 2,499 students packed into less than one-twentieth of a square mile. For real city folks that's nothing, but, to compare, the average for the rest of the state is 5.1 people per square mile.

Scrapping for Stamps
Laramie

Len Austin had an almost wonderful 1972 Volkswagen Bug. It ran fine, but its paint job was in sorry shape. Len could have just gotten the Bug repainted, but instead he opted to cover it with more than 6,000 stamps. He licked each and every stamp, stuck them on, and then shellacked the whole car. After all, he wanted this "paint job" to last. In 1991 Len's car was estimated to be worth $12,000. As the story goes, a few years later Len was in a Kmart parking lot when a stamp collector came up and offered him $20,000 for the stamp car. Turns out some of the stamps Len had used were quite valuable, and because they were shellacked, the philatelist planned on stripping the "paint" and adding it to his stamp collection.

SOUTHEAST

Wyoming Natives
Laramie

Triceratops may be Wyoming's official state dinosaur, but Wyomingites still have a very special place in their hearts for "Big Al," the most complete *Allosaurus* fossil yet found in the world. Big Al, who lived in the Late Jurassic period (which makes him about 145 million years old), was unearthed here in 1991 by a Swiss fossil-collecting company. Unknowingly, the Swiss group, which had permission to work a private parcel of land near Shell, had strayed 200 feet onto public land that was managed by the Bureau of Land Management (BLM). Fossils found on public lands belong to the public, so the BLM quickly mobilized to excavate Big Al (the name given to the fossil by paleontologists working the site).

Big Al (Allosaurus) might not be the state's official dinosaur, but he's certainly a favorite.

Big Al was excavated over eight days that summer, and a skeletal cast—the only skeletal cast of Big Al in existence—was unveiled at the University of Wyoming Geological Museum in 1996. Even ten years after his second birth, Big Al remains a crowd-pleaser. *Allosaurus* could grow to 40 feet long, but Big Al is only 25 feet (paleontologists believe he was a subadult when he died). Despite his relatively small size, his pose is still fearsome: He stands on two powerful hind legs, with a whiplike tail rising from behind, talon-tipped claws on diminutive arms, and a mouth full of razor-sharp teeth.

Allosaurus was the most common large carnivore of the Late Jurassic in North America. It was a predecessor of the better-known *Tyrannosaurus rex* and definitely was not the kind of creature you want to run into. Big Al is the largest, most complete carnivorous dinosaur ever discovered in Wyoming. When he was found, his bones were still in life position.

Big Al's only friends aren't of the human variety. At the UW Geological Museum, he's tail to tail with a contemporary, a giant (70-foot-long) *Brontosaurus*. Mr. Bronto is also a true Wyoming native; he was found 70 miles north of Laramie. While Big Al and the *Brontosaurus* get along well enough now, in life the former ate the latter. *Brontosaurus* is a plant-eating species. Seeing them so close together now, with the *Brontosaurus* dwarfing Big Al, you can see that even with knife-edged teeth and claws, being a hunter in the Jurassic period wasn't easy.

SPEAKING OF DINOS

In 1994 elementary-school students throughout the state chose *Triceratops* as Wyoming's official state dinosaur over three other candidates. Wyoming is one of only two states to have both a state dinosaur and a state fossil. (The state fossil is an obscure small fish.) The world's first *Triceratops* specimen was found in Wyoming in 1887 . . . not that its finders knew what it was. For the first year after its discovery, *Triceratops* was thought to be an extinct type of bison.

The Opposite of Alcatraz

Laramie

The joke is that it was easier for prisoners to get out of Wyoming's Territorial Prison than it was for them to get in. During the thirty years (1872–1902) the prison was in business, it was a temporary home for 13 women and more than 1,000 men. But for 250 of these prisoners—fully 25 percent—it was a much more temporary home than the sentencing judge had planned.

It wasn't that the criminals imprisoned here were escape masterminds. A glance through the records shows that the simple act of a prisoner walking away was more than most guards could prevent. Kind of surprisingly lax security for a federal prison holding some of the region's most notorious outlaws (including Butch Cassidy for a time), isn't it?

A few examples will show that Wyoming's Territorial Prison wasn't exactly a maximum-security facility. Prisoner John Bettle, aka Frank R. Winn, had befriended one of the many antelope that live in this area. With guards' permission, he would go out to feed it each evening. Accustomed to seeing John walk out of the stockades, the guards didn't notice that one evening he just kept walking. The twenty-four-year-old butcher was never recaptured.

Prisoner James Brown was out cleaning the chicken house when the guards got the order to gather up some horses. All of the other convicts were locked up, but James, still in the chicken coop, was forgotten. The wall guard didn't even notice when James just walked away.

The guards weren't totally incompetent, though. Charlie White, a fifty-one-year-old stock dealer from Illinois found guilty of assault with intent to kill, didn't have quite the luck John and James did. By the time Charlie had been at the prison for about a year, guards considered him a reliable fellow and granted him additional privileges around the prison

The prison all the state's lawbreakers hoped to get assigned to.

yard. One day Charlie decided he no longer wanted to cultivate his reliable image, so he walked away. But before he got too far, he was spotted. One guard immediately recognized him as one of their more reliable prisoners and yelled out to his colleagues, "Don't shoot for God's sake, that's Charlie!" The warning wasn't quick enough to stop one guard from getting a shot off. Charlie was hit in the shoulder, taken back to the prison, and tended to by a doctor. Nine months later, the governor pardoned Charlie.

To see the prison convicts hoped they got sent to, exit I–80 at Snowy Range Road and head east for ¼ mile toward downtown Laramie. The prison is on the left. For more information call (307) 745–6161.

STUCK ON A SEAL

The Wyoming state seal was designed in 1891, but it took two years for the state legislature to accept it. Wyoming might have been forward-thinking enough to be the first state or territory to grant women the right to vote, but it still didn't want a naked woman on its state seal. The woman in the original seal design was unclothed. By 1893 the design had her draped, and the state's second legislature finally accepted it.

A Wood-Wood Situation

Laramie

Being the exceedingly windy and snowy place it is, Wyoming has more snow fence than any other state in the country. Constructed upwind of particularly snowy sections of road, snow fences break wind flow and cause snow to be deposited before it reaches the highway and cars pack it down. Not even Wyoming's Department of Transportation knows exactly how much snow fence the state has, but estimates are in the

Wyoming's ubiquitous snow fence, before and after reclamation.

millions of linear feet. The highest concentrations of snow fence are along I–80 and in the northeast part of the state.

Snow fences don't last forever, though. Depending on where they are and how badly they are beaten by wind and snow, snow fences are usually ready for retirement after about ten years. Seeing an opportunity, local entrepreneurs John Pope and Sandi Johnson came up with a second career for snow fence: as decor for homes and businesses. You can find reclaimed Wyoming snow fence adorning the interior walls of several East Coast Red Lobster restaurants and a McDonald's franchise in Florida; homeowners in some twenty U.S. states as well as in Japan have bought Wyoming snow fence for use as siding, wainscoting, and interior paneling and to make cabinets and furniture.

It's like reclaimed barn wood, only better, because snow fence is completely natural—no dyes, paints, or stains—and standardized. Every piece is 1 inch by 6 inches by 16 feet. Coming from low-humidity Wyoming, the wood has a low moisture content. Sitting out in severe weather that usually includes several car-burying blizzards every winter, snow fence is as weathered in ten years as a barn is in a century.

Centennial Woods, the company John and Sandi founded and which is now run by President and CEO Gene Klawetter, doesn't just rip down ready-for-retirement snow fences; the company also replaces each and every fir or pine board that it removes. In fact, Centennial Woods was initially able to get its snow-fence-farming contract from the Wyoming Department of Transportation (WYDOT), the organization responsible for erecting and maintaining the fence, because unauthorized people had been stealing fence boards without replacing them.

"These poachers would strip the snow fence wood without permission at night and wouldn't replace what they had taken. Snow fences were disappearing, and this would cause problems along roads," Gene says. John and Sandi went to WYDOT with a win-win proposition: They would remove old snow fence boards and replace them with new, raw, rough-cut wood of the same type and size. "Replacing what we remove gives us an unlimited supply that will last forever," says Gene. "Here in Wyoming, the wind is going to continue to blow, and it will continue to snow."

Check out Centennial Woods online at www.centennialwoods.com.

A Man, His Mule, and a Newspaper
Laramie

I haven't yet decided if it's stranger that Laramie's only daily paper is named after an animal or that the animal it is named after is a mule, given that Laramie is smack in the middle of horse and cattle country.

Edgar Wilson Nye, also known as Bill Nye and one of the most famous comic writers of his time, founded the *Daily Boomerang* in March 1881. He named it in memory of a favorite mule, Boomerang. Boomerang the mule seems to have come by his name rightly. He had the habit of following Bill into bars, only to be shooed away and then return "just like a boomerang."

Since Bill was a humorist, maybe he named his paper in memory of his mule for laughs . . . or maybe he was just really attached to Boomerang. But that isn't all Bill did in memory of Boomerang. Bill's 1881 book, *Bill Nye and Boomerang; or The Tale of a Meek-Eyed Mule and Some Other Literary Gems*, was dedicated to Boomerang:

To My Mule Boomerang,

Whose bright smile haunts me still, and whose low, mellow notes are ever sounding in my ears to whom I owe all that I am as a great man, and whose presence has inspired me ever and anon throughout the years that are gone.

Bill obviously had an affinity for embellished prose. Before immortalizing Boomerang and founding his paper, Bill had to resign as postmaster of a Laramie post office. He sent his letter of resignation directly to President Garfield. After several paragraphs alerting the president of various minutiae in and about the Laramie post office—the safe combination, the location of unused postal card stock—Bill ended his letter in grand style:

> Mr. President, as an official of this Government I now retire. My term of office would not expire until 1886. I must, therefore, beg pardon for my eccentricity in resigning. It will be best, perhaps, to keep the heart-breaking news from the ears of European powers until the dangers of a financial panic are fully past. Then hurl it broadcast with a sickening thud.

Seems Mr. Nye and the bar-hopping Boomerang were characters meant for each other. To this day the *Boomerang* runs a cartoon sketch of its notable namesake as its logo.

The only newspaper named after a mule.

Keeping the Wild West Alive

Laramie

A few Wyoming towns have been staging fake shootouts for the amusement of visitors since the 1950s. As recently as 1971 Laramie has had a real Wild West shootout, with a real gun and real bullets, and inspired by real unrequited love. Proof of it remains today: The mirror behind the bar in the Buckhorn has a hole in it. If you look closely you'll notice the hole is just about the size of a bullet.

Charlie Phillips, a regular at the Buckhorn, had a bit of a crush on one of the barmaids, Nedra. The evening of the shootout, he came into the Buckhorn to flirt with Nedra as usual. As usual, Nedra didn't warm up to Charlie's advances and didn't really encourage him.

Charlie left. But then he came back . . . just in time to see Nedra, now off duty, saddled up to the bar and sitting at the bar next to some other guy. Nedra pecked this other guy on the cheek while Charlie was watching. Infuriated, and drunk, Charlie rushed out to his car and grabbed a gun. He came back in and fired a shot into the ceiling. Everyone scattered, and Charlie left. He didn't make it too far, though.

The bullet hole in the mirror.

Now out in the middle of the street in front of the Buckhorn, Charlie fired a few more shots into the air before turning his attention back to the bar. He fired a shot right through the front window. No one can remember what happened to the window itself, but legend has it that Charlie's bullet took out the "C" in the neon Coors sign before piercing a perfect hole through the mirror. Because this was a real shootout, naturally it was real law enforcement that came after Charlie. He might not have technically broken a mirror, but Charlie still ended up with at least seven years of bad luck. (He was carted off to jail.) The Buckhorn ended up with the most famous mirror in the state. No one knows where Nedra ended up.

The Buckhorn and its hole-y mirror are at 114 East Ivinson. Call (307) 742–3554 for more information.

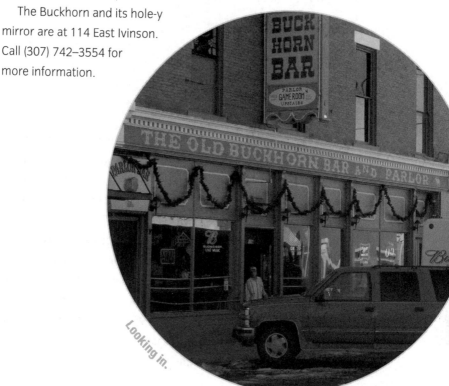

Looking in.

WELL READ

Benjamin Franklin might have founded The Library Company of Philadelphia in 1731, but it wasn't at all like the free libraries we all know and love today. Individuals had to buy "shares" in order to borrow books. It took another 155 years—and a move of about 3,000 miles west—before the country's first public county library system, the library system in most widespread use today, was created in Laramie County.

Try Not to Get Lost
Lost Springs

It is the smallest incorporated municipality in the United States, but it is bigger than the sign (POPULATION 1) welcoming you to town indicates. Lost Springs has four residents: Mayor Leda Price; council members Arthur Stringham and Clara Stringham, who is Arthur's mother; and Arthur's brother Alfred Stringham.

Even though Lost Springs is but four people these days, the town still has a post office, which makes the town not only the smallest municipality in the United States but also the smallest U.S. town with a post office. The post office, with postmaster Rona Bruegger manning just under fifty rural and rented boxes from 9:00 A.M. to noon six days a week, shares space with the Stringhams' antiques store. In May 2006 Rona got nearly a dozen new customers when the post office in neighboring Shawnee closed.

Lost Springs didn't always require its buildings to pull double duty. Named by railroad workers who couldn't find a spring their maps said was right here, the town was once big enough to support a church-affiliated college-prep high school, a two-year junior college, a few bars, and several businesses. But then the nearby Lance Creek oil boom, which kept more than 150 Lost Springers employed, went bust, and Jireh College closed. All that remains of the college today are a few crumbled bricks and a stone with the college's name on it. By 1969, when the Stringhams moved to Lost Springs from their outlying ranch, Lost Springs had already lost enough residents that they doubled the town's population.

Even though some people might be bothered that the nearest grocery store is 30 miles away, the local bar is usually only open on weekends and during hunting season, and the round-trip commute to their job is 120 miles (as Arthur's is), Arthur says he likes Lost Springs just fine. "It's quiet and there's no crime."

Wide-Open Spaces
Lusk

In 1918 Lusk had a population close to 10,000. Today, the town has just under 1,500 residents. Its elevation is more than three times that! Still, because Lusk is the county seat of the least populated county (Niobrara) in the least populated state (Wyoming has just over 500,000 residents; for comparison, neighboring Colorado has 4,300,000), it is a local megalopolis.

About half of the 3,000 residents of Niobrara County call Lusk home. Lusk has the only grocery store, bank, school, and hardware store for miles around. Even including the relatively crowded commercial streets of Lusk, Niobrara County's population density is one person per 524 acres. According to the 2000 census, New York County, the country's most densely populated, has one person per 0.009 acre.

> ## DRINK UP!
> Put simply, Lusk has quite the thermos. A giant redwood tank was built here in 1886 to store and dispense water to the steam engines of the Fremont Elkhorn & Missouri Valley Railroad. Although it hasn't quenched the thirst of passing trains for years, the tank received a major refurbishment between 1971 and 1986.

Memorializing a Madam
Lusk

The nation's capital honors presidents and soldiers with the Washington Monument, the Lincoln Memorial, and the Vietnam Memorial. South Dakota celebrates corn with the Corn Palace. Saratoga, New York, has a monument to Benedict Arnold's leg. From serious to silly, America abounds with memorials and monuments. Even so, Wyoming has found one person and one profession to immortalize that no other state has. Just outside Lusk sits a 3,500-pound pink-granite slab honoring a prostitute.

Mother Featherlegs came to Wyoming Territory in 1876 and opened a saloon and brothel on the Cheyenne-Deadwood Stage Road. She became quite prosperous, not to mention a favorite among men, despite her not-all-that-attractive-sounding nickname. Mother Featherlegs, aka Charlotte Shephard, would often ride astride her horse at a gallop across the prairie, her lace-trimmed red pantalettes flapping in the wind. One man remarked on the similarity between a galloping Charlotte and a feather-legged chicken to a friend, and she was forever after known as Mother Featherlegs.

Unfortunately, she wasn't Mother Featherlegs in life for too much longer. In 1879, just three years after her arrival in Wyoming, Mother Featherlegs's slain body was found near a spring close to her house. It was thought that one of her business partners, Dangerous Dick, had murdered her and skipped town with her cache of money and jewelry. Years later, when Dangerous Dick was arrested for another crime and was about to be hanged in Louisiana, he confessed to having killed Mother Featherlegs.

The monument was paid for and erected by locals in Mother's honor in 1964. (One of the monument's funders has even saved himself and his wife a burial plot next to the monument.) The day the monument was dedicated in front of a crowd of 750, the red pantalettes that earned Mother Featherlegs her nickname were on display. That night, however, they were stolen. In 1990 the pantalettes surfaced in a Deadwood, South Dakota, saloon. Almost immediately, a posse of Lusk residents, determined to bring the undergarments of their famous Featherlegs back home, raided the place. Not wanting to run the risk of their being stolen again, Lusk now keeps Mother Featherlegs's pantalettes at its Stagecoach Museum (322 South Main; 307–334–3444).

An unlikely monument to the world's oldest profession.

BARBIE BUSH

At the Stagecoach Museum in Lusk, you can meet every First Lady from Martha Washington through Barbara Bush in their inaugural finery. Local craftswoman and seamstress Helen Davies recreated the exact outfit that each First Lady wore to her husband's inaugural ball . . . in Barbie-doll scale. The Inaugural Barbie collection stops at Barbara Bush because Helen died in January 1994. The museum is still looking for someone to keep the tradition going.

It's the Pits

Manville

Nowadays it's not unusual to find Wyoming products—everything from agate to natural gas to trona—throughout the country, and even the world. Between interstates, trains, and planes, getting bits and pieces of Wyoming out to the rest of the world is a breeze. But what about 10,000 years ago? You'd think that with hand delivery via foot travel being the only option, Wyoming materials would have stayed close to home. Spanish Diggings, a very ancient archaeological site, proves otherwise, though.

Beginning 10,000 years ago, pits 30 feet deep were dug here with stone tools. Quartzite, jasper, and agate mined from these pits—which dot a 400-square-mile area—have been found as far afield as the Ohio and Mississippi Valleys. In addition to the quarries, there are other signs of Paleo-Indian life, such as tepee rings, hearths, and chipping stations. Even though the site's name would seem to indicate some Spanish involvement over its long history, that is not the case. The cowboy who discovered the site in 1879 thought Spaniards had dug for gold here and named it accordingly. By the time archaeologists realized the cowboy was wrong, it was too late: The name had already stuck.

Spanish Diggings can be found down Spanish Diggings Road, off U.S. Highway 18/20, between Lost Springs and Manville.

Taking Initiative
Pine Bluffs

Marjorie Trefren of Cheyenne had no idea she would forever alter the vista along I–80 by Pine Bluffs when she returned from a trip to European Catholic shrines and churches in 1991. Back home, however, intrigued by all she had seen in Europe, she became interested in Catholic shrines closer to home. Well, she tried to become interested in them . . . until she realized that Wyoming had no Catholic shrines. It was a situation that she and her husband, Ted, hoped to change.

The couple began looking for suitable land, where the shrine would be easily seen. Eventually they settled on five acres just off I–80 on the eastern edge of Pine Bluffs, a town of just over 1,000 people and where archaeological digs have shown human occupation dating back 10,000 years. Finding the land wasn't the hardest part of the project, though. Looking for a sculptor, Marjorie and Ted queried monument companies across the country, but no one seemed right for the project. Finally, perhaps out of desperation, the couple tried something much simpler: They opened the Cheyenne Yellow Pages. Talking with Cheyenne sculptor Robert Fida, Marjorie and Ted knew they had found their man.

Robert sculpted a 6-foot-tall Virgin Mary that Marjorie and Ted approved. That was just the beginning, though. The final sculpture was to be 30 feet tall, a scale that makes the statue highly visible. Robert developed laser technology that took measurements from the mini-Mary and then used these measurements to create a computer-generated foam enlargement. (Where do you get that much foam?) Next, pieces of fiberglass created to hold concrete were molded on the foam. When finished, the fiberglass mold was assembled and filled with concrete made from ground white marble. Our Lady of Peace, unveiled in October 1998, is one of the largest statues of the Virgin Mary in the United States.

You probably won't need directions to view the sculpture. If you drive along I–80, or pretty much any street in Pine Bluffs, there's no way to miss a 30-foot-tall gleaming white statue.

The Tree Is Mightier Than the Train
Sherman Hill

It's hard to imagine a little pine tree determining the course of a train, but that's just what happened between 1867 and 1869 when the Union Pacific Railroad was laying tracks in this area. Fascinated by a twisted tree growing out of a solid rock, builders from the railroad are rumored to have diverted the tracks slightly to leave the miracle tree unmolested. After the tracks were down and trains were zipping back and forth across the country, trains would stop here, both so passengers could wonder at the marvel of a tree growing out of solid rock and so train engineers and firemen could water it. I guess they figured that a tree growing out of bare rock could use all the help it could get. Eventually the railroad men even wrapped a steel cable around the tree's rock to keep it from splitting.

Trains stopped passing by Tree Rock in 1901, but today the interstate goes right by it. (The Wyoming Department of Transportation made the decision to build around the tree as well.) The exact age of the tree is unknown, but limber pine can live as long as 2,000 years. The rock the tree calls home is between one and four billion years old. Tree Rock sits in between east and west I–80 near mile marker 332.

Pyramid on the Prairie
Near Sherman Hill

Ames Monument has been called one of the finest memorials in the country, and other projects by the same prominent architect are gazed upon by multitudes on a daily basis. For these reasons alone, you would think there would be lines, or at least a small crowd, coming to see the monument every day. But no. A granite pyramid 60 feet by 60 feet at its base and 60 feet tall, Ames Monument is fortunate to get a few dozen visitors a week.

Henry Hobson Richardson's pyramid-shaped memorial to the Ames brothers, the two men responsible for securing much of the financing

A giant pyramid . . . with no crowds lined up to see it.

that made the transcontinental railroad possible, wasn't always so over-looked. In 1881, when the Union Pacific Railroad paid $65,000 to honor the Ames brothers with this pyramid, the monument lay right along the transcontinental rail route and marked the railroad's highest point.

Every UP passenger traveling through Wyoming could look at the Ames Monument and notice the similarities it shared with Boston's Trinity Church, the Allegheny County Courthouse (Pennsylvania), and numerous libraries throughout New England, all also designed by Richardson. But then in 1901 the railroad was rerouted several miles to the south, and this monument was left alone on the Wyoming prairie. Because of its height and the fact that it's made completely from giant, rough-hewn granite blocks quarried from Reeds Rock, ½ mile to the west, there's no chance of the monument being relocated anytime soon. You'll just have to take my word that it's worth the five-minute detour off I–80.

Although you would think a pyramid of this size, rising out of an empty plain, is difficult to miss, you might find basic directions helpful. Take exit 329 from I–80 and then head south for 1 mile or so.

WYOMING GEOMETRY

Wyoming is one of only three states entirely bounded by straight lines. The other two are Utah and Colorado.

SOUTHEAST

A Horse of a Different Age
North of Torrington

Babe was anything but a babe when she died at the ripe old age of fifty-two, which, for a horse, is just shy of a world's record. Up until she died, Babe was the world's oldest living horse. Born in April 1906 in South Dakota, Babe was bought from an abusive owner by a Goshen County couple, Velda and Wayne Childers, in 1936. At that point Babe was already at the typical thirty-year equine life span. No doubt thinking Babe might already be on her last legs, Velda and Wayne wanted to make her final years as comfortable as possible. They spared nothing when nursing the 37-inch-tall, 330-pound black-and-white Shetland back to health. With each passing year, both Velda and Wayne and the Goshen County community were pleasantly surprised that Babe was doing so well. While Babe's age was certainly noteworthy, the Childerses and area community loved Babe, nicknamed "Little Sweetheart of the Prairie," for her personality and intelligence.

Somewhere in her late forties, Babe began to attract national attention, and by age fifty she was receiving visitors from around the world who would stop by Velda and Wayne's home to pay their respects. Up until she died on June 14, 1958, Babe remained active and had good eyesight and hearing. She was buried, and a monument was erected in her honor. The monument sits on private land, but the owners generally agree when visitors want to visit Babe. Here in Wyoming, we know how important horses are, even when they're in horse heaven.

From Paris to Wyoming
Van Tassel

After members of the American Expeditionary Force founded the American Legion in Paris in 1919, Van Tassel wasted no time in getting the state's, and the country's, first Legion Post up and running. The first meeting was held June 28, 1919. During that meeting it was decided that the Van Tassel Post would be named in honor of Ferdinand Branstetter, one of the first Van Tassel men serving in World War I to fall in action. Branstetter had come to Wyoming from Nebraska a few years before the war and filed a homestead south of the town.

While the Branstetter Post was the first in the country, today there are 15,000 American Legion Posts around the world; each state has at least one, and there are several in foreign countries. But it is little Van Tassel that has Post No. 1.

Putting a Spring in Your Step
Woods Landing

Don't be surprised if you pull out some new dance moves on the floor at the Woods Landing Bar and Dance Hall. Perhaps someone figured that the area's cowboys and ranchers needed as much help getting their groove on as possible, because when this dance hall was built in the late 1920s or early 1930s, springs were put in the floor. The entirety of the floor's 40-by-60-foot space sits atop old boxcar springs.

Owners Sue Spencer and husband Bill Sheehan recently added a patio to the building. During this expansion they had planned on digging down far enough to see the springs for themselves and even build a little "observation window." Unfortunately, it didn't work because they would have had to dig down too far. Sadly, you'll just have to settle on feeling, rather than seeing, the springs.

Sue says that when enough people are out there dancing—and there are still dances most Saturday nights throughout the summer as well as key winter days like New Year's Eve and Valentine's Day—the bounce is certainly palpable. Good thing, too; today, in addition to the real-life ranchers who still pop in, vacationing dudes sore from spending more time on the back of a horse than they are used to show up to shake a leg. These poor guys and gals really do need all the help they can get.

The Woods Landing Bar and Dance Hall is in downtown Woods Landing. Call (307) 745–9638 for more information.

This dance floor looks innocuous, but springs hidden underneath take dancers for a ride.

NORTHEAST

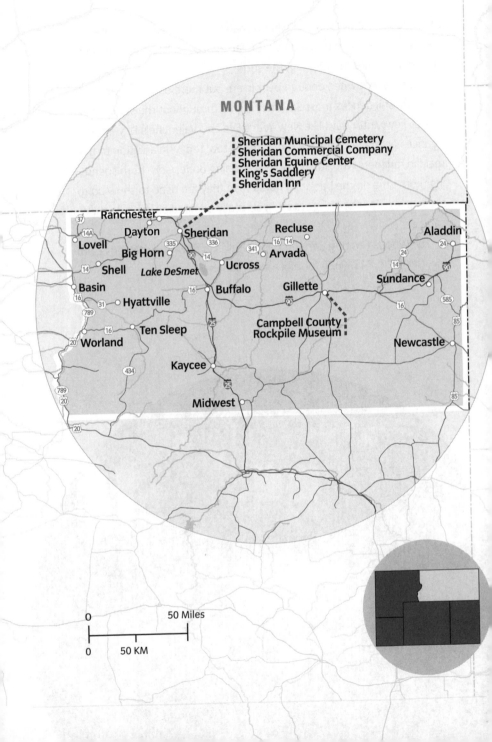

MONTANA

Sheridan Municipal Cemetery
Sheridan Commercial Company
Sheridan Equine Center
King's Saddlery
Sheridan Inn

Ranchester
Dayton
Lovell
Big Horn
Shell
Basin
Hyattville
Worland
Ten Sleep
Kaycee
Midwest

Sheridan
Recluse
Arvada
Ucross
Buffalo
Gillette

Aladdin
Sundance
Newcastle

Lake DeSmet

Campbell County
Rockpile Museum

0   50 Miles

0   50 KM

NORTHEAST

Butch Cassidy, the Sundance Kid, Frank and Jesse James—they all loved northeastern Wyoming. Even though some of the area's biggest draws—the only spot in the country where it's legal to do a U-turn on a bridge, an animal hospital that gives horses new legs, and a library that consists only of cupboards—weren't yet around, the outlaws still managed to keep themselves busy here . . . even if they were most often busy with hiding out in secret caves. Those secret caves, including the famous Hole in the Wall, are still here and welcome visitors, but I'd rather search out the terrible, terrifying Smettie, a town that can't seem to make up its mind as to exactly where it wants to be, or even a good helping of miracle mud.

Everything Including the Kitchen Sink
Aladdin

It's no wonder the Aladdin General Store sells everything from clothing to fishing supplies, groceries, art, antiques, beer, and hardware. After all, it has been collecting inventory since 1896 and today has a base of only fifteen regular customers. (That'd be the entire town of Aladdin, which was named after the *Arabian Nights* character in hopes of bringing good luck and riches.) I bet some of the "antiques" weren't yet antique when they first came to the store.

While the Aladdin General Store's inventory has probably changed a bit over the last century, little else has. Well, an icebox was added to the front porch by the "Liar's Bench"—a gathering place for tellers of tall tales—a while ago. The interior woodwork, cabinetry, and windows are all original. The peeling wallpaper upstairs in "Aladdin's Antique Attic" is original. The roll-top storage bins behind the counter are original . . . and old scribblings on them bear proof of rising prices over the years. There's even a twenty-four-hour windup clock . . . not that owners Judy or Rick Brengle remember to wind it all that much.

One very welcome recent change is the addition of bacon to the store's list of available groceries. The Brengles get it in slabs from a North Dakota producer and cut it into thick slices themselves. Tourists are warned not to try it but rarely follow that advice. "It's addictive," says Judy. "They'll find themselves driving back here for more."

The store, the best-preserved of Wyoming's five remaining nineteenth-century mercantiles, happily keeps accounts for Aladdin locals (who can eat as much bacon as they choose). "You certainly can't do that at Wal-Mart," Judy says. The Aladdin General Store (307–896–2226; www.aladdinwy.com) is hard to miss in downtown Aladdin.

HIGH LOW

At 3,740 feet above sea level, Aladdin is Wyoming's lowest-elevation settlement. So take a deep breath and enjoy the thickest air in the state.

Last Stand

Arvada

By the early 1880s Wyoming's wild bison were in trouble; as a result of hunting, their population had fallen from more than 100,000 to only a few dozen. By 1884 it was pretty much over for them: That year, one of the last known wild bison was killed outside of Arvada.

Moreton Frewen, an Englishman who ranched in the area, spotted the lone bison from a window in his ranch house one summer afternoon. He wrote in his diary, "I ran into the hall, not even half dressed, picked an Express rifle out of the rack and broke the poor brute's shoulder, killing him 10 minutes later on the flat a quarter of a mile away." Thankfully, realizing that bison were heading the way of the woolly mammoth, the American Bison Society was founded in 1905 to prevent the creature's extinction. In 1908 a wild herd of twenty-one bison were settled in Yellowstone National Park. Today, that herd is more than 4,000 strong and is the largest free-ranging bison herd in the United States.

Just Add Water

Basin

Wyoming's Great Basin, of which the town of Basin is rather the epicenter, got its name for a reason: It is the driest part of the state and receives an average of only 5 to 8 inches of rain annually. If you visit Basin from late May to mid-June, however, you'd never guess this. Thanks to well-planned irrigation canals and a citywide drive starting in the early twentieth century, the town is full of blooming lilac bushes. So full, in fact, that the lilacs outnumber residents by more than a factor of four! Basin has over 5,000 lilacs and only 1,200 residents.

It's amazing what can grow with a little water.

Now, not to pick a fight, but Basin is a tiny town in the country's least populated state, and another U.S. city has taken advantage of its remoteness to advance its own flora. When I mentioned Basin's quiet claim of having more lilacs than any other city in the country to my mother, she, having already been brainwashed by this other city's slick marketing machine, replied, "Rochester might have something to say about that." Well, little Basin has something to say to Rochester: "You've got nothing on us!" (Not that anyone in Basin would be that confrontational.)

Rochester, New York, has a mere 1,200 lilac bushes. Still, it holds The Lilac Festival every year. That's right; capital "T" on *The* Lilac Festival. No "Rochester Lilac Festival" or "Highland Park Lilac Festival," but just plain "The Lilac Festival," as if no other town can compare. Oddly, Basin residents, even when they're out pruning the lilacs in their front yards, don't seem to mind. They're still perfectly content with the Sears Foundation's 1933 christening of their town as "Lilac Capital of the World."

Stomping the Divots

Big Horn

This might be cowboy country, but here in Big Horn, the cowboys are a little different: They play polo . . . at one of the largest, most storied, and most successful polo clubs in the country. In fact, the horses at Big Horn Polo Club often outnumber the human residents of the town (whose population is around 217).

Founded at the end of the nineteenth century by the Moncrieffe brothers, and supported by nobility from Scotland who followed the brothers to this area, the Big Horn Polo Club is home to the headquarters and breeding operations of two of the last three U.S. Open winners. The first man to umpire a polo game here was a personal friend of

Crazy Horse. The Moncrieffe brothers were so enamored with the game that they even required their cowhands to learn how to play.

Nowadays, players come from all over the world—Argentina, Great Britain, India, South Africa, Australia, Florida—both to play and to look over some of the best-blooded untrained and trained prospects in the world. Big Horn horses can be found on fields from Palermo to Saratoga. One of the two bars in town has walls adorned with photos of close to one hundred of these visiting players and buyers.

Even though polo has a long history in Big Horn, concessions are made to the area's cowboy culture. Games are sometimes played in the mornings to make room for steer ropers in the afternoon. Rival dude ranchers play an annual game of Cowboy Polo, slightly less technical than real polo: Equipment includes brooms and a volleyball. About a decade ago, one of the dude ranch crews boycotted this event—the reasons why have been lost to history—and was replaced by a team of Crow Indians. With the Crow, as usual, riding bareback and requesting that the cowboys do the same, it was an interesting take on the "Cowboys and Indians" game so many of us played as kids. Without their saddles, most of the cowboys were off their horses and on the ground in less than three minutes.

If you're planning to be in Big Horn for a spell, the polo club (307–751–6969; www.thebighornpoloclub.com) has a school that is totally free to the public. Just want to catch a game? Practice games are at 3:00 and 5:00 P.M. every Wednesday and Friday and at 10:00 A.M. on Sunday. It's always a good idea to call ahead to double-check. Tournament games are usually at 2:00 P.M. on Sunday but are sometimes scheduled for weekdays or Saturday to accommodate visiting players.

Miracle Mud

Bighorn Mountains

Now, I learned about bentonite's unique properties my first summer in Wyoming. The Teton County Fair stipulated bentonite, and only bentonite, as the proper substance in which to pig-wrestle. Being a child of the Maryland suburbs who had never seen, much less tussled with, swine, of course I signed up to pig-wrestle faster than you could say "oink." I quickly learned that bentonite was mandated for additional audience enjoyment: It was slicker than any other kind of clay I had previously encountered. It was amazing. Almost as amazing as my sorry pig-wrestling performance. (I blame it all on the bentonite.) As it turns out, however, there is a subclass of bentonite that is even more amazing than the stuff used in the wrestling ring.

It was a trapper working in the Bighorn Mountains who first discovered pascalite, a calcium-based bentonite that was eventually named after him, in the 1930s. While tending to his traps along the shores of a remote lake, trapper Pascal's chapped hands got coated in a whitish, cheeselike substance. Rather than plunge his dirty hands into the freezing lake, Pascal let the clay dry and washed it off back at his cabin. To his surprise, his chapped hands seemed to be less chapped. He and some friends spent the next few years experimenting with the clay and decided it was nothing short of miraculous.

Today, pascalite is mined deep in the Bighorn Mountains, in a secluded, high-vortex area at an elevation of nearly 9,000 feet above sea level, and not far from Pascal's lake. It has been found nowhere else in the world. A private company mines the pascalite, dries it, and sells it in powder, capsule, and numerous other forms. Not that Pascal and his friends were able to figure all this out, but pascalite supposedly cures everything from brown recluse spider bites to burns, infections, ulcers, cystic acne, skin cancer, and eye cataracts. And because no one wants to smell bad, even when they're just getting on the road to good health, pascalite can also be used as deodorant.

Of course no scientific studies back up any of these claims, but the list of testimonials from satisfied customers is long. A doctor has testified in court that pascalite is the only known cure for a brown recluse spider bite. One person suffering from an active ulcer and hyperacidity took two capsules four times a day, and all symptoms were gone in a week. Pascalite is reported to have natural antibiotic and analgesic properties. Beauticians have stated that there's no facial product that can compare. Pascalite's skin-tightening effects (when used on the face) can be so strong as to even be painful. I see a new pascalite product: Bighorn Botox.

MULTITALENTED MAYOR

In the same year that Ernest Rutherford discovered the structure of the atom, the Ottawa Senators won the Stanley Cup, and the first feature film was screened—that'd be 1911—Dayton became the first community in the state to elect a woman mayor. Despite continuing with her millinery and dry-goods store during her first term, Susan Wissler was so successful in her political position that she was elected to a second term. In doing so, she became the first woman mayor in the country to serve two consecutive terms. She still didn't give up her store, though.

Daredevil Driving
Buffalo

You know you've always wanted to do it. Possibly even dreamed about doing it. Well, there's no better place to do it than Buffalo, so go for it. "It," of course, being a U-turn in the middle of a bridge on a U.S. highway. Buffalo is the perfect place for it because it's the only place in the entire country where such daredevil driving won't result in a ticket, or even a scolding from local law enforcement. Making a U-turn on the U.S. Highway 16 bridge over Clear Creek is perfectly legal . . . but you don't need to tell that little detail to your friends back home.

It's surprising there isn't more signage announcing this as the unique bridge it is.

PLENTY OF PUBLIC LAND

The federal government owns 50 percent of Wyoming's 97,818 square miles. The state owns another 6 percent of the land.

Calling It What It Is

Gillette

Gillette has what very well may be one of the best natural landmarks ever: a giant pile of rocks—I'm talking house-size here—just off Second Street. It's always been there, and no one knows how all the rocks got there. The mystery doesn't stop locals from using it when giving directions to most anywhere: "Take a right past the giant rock pile and then we're the third house on the left" or "Take a left at the first intersection past the rock pile."

When Campbell County acquired a property for the purpose of housing the county museum at the foot of the rock pile in the 1970s, the name of the new museum wasn't discussed for too long. Wyoming sensibility pretty much mandated "Rockpile Museum." The museum has absolutely nothing to do with rocks, but the namers figured that didn't matter so much as being able to find the place. Rockpile Museum it was.

Although the museum doesn't have any rocks, it does have some interesting exhibits showcasing the region's history, much of which has to do with coal mining—more than one-quarter of the country's coal

The rock pile is exactly what you would expect.

supplies come from a 60-mile radius of here—and ranching. Although not always on display, an interesting collection shows the evolution of barbed wire. If you're the first person in recorded history unable to locate the giant rock pile, look for 900 West Second Street. Or call (307) 682–5723 and ask for directions.

A Real Neck Strainer
Gillette

The neck-craning wonders Wyoming is best known for might be mountains, but, even so, something here has to hold the record for being the state's tallest man-made structure. While the sky-kissing, twelve-story White Hall on the University of Wyoming campus is Wyoming's tallest residential structure, Gillette's 700-foot-tall LORAN antenna is, without a doubt, the state's tallest structure of any kind. Still, our antenna is not even half the height of New York City's Empire State Building (which isn't even anywhere near that city's tallest structure anymore). Owned by the U.S. Coast Guard, the Gillette antenna, as part of the nationwide LORAN network, helps with maritime navigation. Never mind that it is many, many miles from any ocean. These days, however, the LORAN system is largely being replaced by global positioning system technology.

But even when the antenna becomes obsolete and is taken down, White Hall still won't be able to remove the adjective "residential" from its height title. No, there's not another tall antenna out there, but there is a power plant. The Jim Bridger Power Plant, opened in the 1970s 25 miles east of Rock Springs in the southwestern part of the state, has a smokestack that soars twenty-four stories into the heavens.

Living Up to Expectations
Northeast of Hyattville

Lighting might be a problem, but if officials could figure that out, you could have three football games going on, end to end and all at once, inside the Great Expectations cave. The third-deepest limestone cave in the country, Great Expectations (or Great X, as it's known in the speleological community) is home to the Great Hall, which is 1,000 feet long and 100 feet tall. It's one of the largest rooms in a cave in the country.

While the Great Hall is certainly spacious, not all of Great X is. Just before the cave's exit is the aptly named "Grim Crawl of Death" a 1,500-foot-long, water-logged passage that you've got no choice but to negotiate on your belly. Author and National Speleological Society expedition leader Michael Ray Taylor calls this terrifying, technical section "the Eiger of caving." Just don't tell the football players. Chances are the defensive linemen couldn't even squeeze themselves through! Great X is 16 miles northeast of Hyattville on dirt roads. Only experienced cavers with a permit should attempt to enter the cave.

FINDING THE ONE PLACE THE LAW WOULDN'T LOOK

While most criminals want to break out of jail, one burglar broke into the Kaycee Jail. In 1950, after breaking into a saloon and grocery store, a man escaped with his loot into the first unlocked building he found, the Kaycee Jail. While officers throughout the state were looking for him everywhere but behind bars, the man enjoyed his stolen liquor and food. He was finally discovered after several days and taken to the Buffalo Jail, where he complained that the Kaycee Jail was much nicer.

Thinking Out of the Box
Kaycee

Back in the day when the state was still being settled, it wasn't unusual for a saloon to be the first structure to go up in a town. George Peterson built Kaycee's first saloon/building out of logs in 1897, and within a decade it defined the town. Literally. In 1906 the Wyoming legislature passed a bill stating that only incorporated places could have saloons. Kaycee was not yet incorporated. Area residents weren't ready to shutter their saloon, so they set about incorporating themselves, which wasn't too hard . . . with one exception.

In order to be incorporated, a town needed to have 250 residents. Kaycee, however, barely had 150 people, so it was forced to get creative. If the corporate limits were extended 20 miles in every direction, the "town" did have a population of 250. This new, improved, supersize Kaycee had no problems incorporating. The saloon remained popular with the residents of both near and far Kaycee until it burned down in 1928.

Making a Quick Exit
Kaycee

Tardy bookworms had the perfect setup at the old Kaycee Branch Library. A trap door leading to a gully outside allowed them to escape any overdue fines. No one knows for sure who built the trap door, but it is suspected that Deputy Sheriff Leonard Beard—who lived in the building in the 1890s, when the area was a hotbed of outlaw activity—was the responsible party.

Anxious to collect the rewards for as many outlaws as possible, Beard had more than a few enemies; it was prudent for him to not always make his whereabouts known. Besides Beard's sneaking away from angry outlaws and bookworms sneaking out on fines, this building also allowed city officials to sneak out for whatever reason—it was the Kaycee city hall for much of the first part of the twentieth century.

In 1952 the library moved in and took only sixteen years to outgrow the space. Even though the library could have expanded by constructing a connecting building accessed through the trap door, officials opted for a completely new, non-trap-door building instead. The old library is now part of the Hoofprints of the Past Museum and is used for museum classes. You can find the museum at 344 Nolan Avenue. For more information call (307) 738–2381.

It Would Have Been a Nice Place to Retire

Kern

In 1936, eight years after becoming the first woman to fly across the Atlantic and a year before setting out on her flight around the world, Amelia Earhart came to the tiny hamlet of Kern . . . and loved it so much that she started building her dream retirement home here. She didn't care that she wasn't yet forty. Earhart felt that she only "had one good flight left in" her; she knew retirement wasn't going to be that far away. After she disappeared over the Pacific with 22,000 miles of the circumnavigation under her belt and a mere 7,000 miles to go, construction on Earhart's dream home ended. A few partially finished walls still stand a rough and long 2 miles past the Brown Mountain Campground, which itself is 25 miles southwest of Meeteetse on the Wood River Road. Doing what it could to bring Earhart's dreams of retiring in the area to fruition, the town of Meeteetse erected a monument in her honor in 1972.

Scotland Has Nothing on Lake DeSmet
Lake DeSmet

Scotland might have the fearsome Loch Ness Monster and Maryland's Chesapeake Bay has Chessie, but both pale in comparison to the utterly terrifying Smettie, described by the few local ranchers who have lived to tell the tale as a "30- to 40-foot-long telephone pole with a lard bucket for a head." Other reported characteristics include a "bony ridge along the back, with a resemblance to a horse's head coming out of the water with a swimming motion." Scary indeed.

These waters look benign, but there's a monster lurking beneath.

Teddi Schumacher, a lifetime Lake DeSmet local, has actually seen Smettie more times than she can remember and describes it a bit differently: "It's like four circles in a line, with the two in the middle the biggest, coming out of the water." Not enough of a description? Teddi will happily draw it for you. If you ask nicely, she'll even point out the spot where she's seen the beast (it's always in the same area, easily visible through the window of The Lake Stop, where she works every summer).

Smettie is said to dwell in not-yet-discovered subterranean caverns, which some think might be outlets to the faraway (very faraway) Pacific Ocean. While I can't guarantee that a visit to Lake DeSmet will result in your seeing Smettie (and who can blame it for remaining hidden? Would you want to be seen in public if you were described as looking like a telephone pole with a lard bucket for a head?), it is a great place for fishing, so be sure to take a rod if you go.

LIGHTS, CAMERA, TOUCHDOWN!

A company town established by Midwest Oil Company in the 1920s, Midwest didn't take long to distinguish itself: In 1925 Midwest was the site of the first evening interscholastic football game played under artificial lights in the country.

It's a Bird! It's a Plane! It's a Modern Way to Round Up Horses!
North of Lovell

Sure, raised wooden sidewalks may no longer be strictly necessary (as western streets are no longer covered in horse droppings), and outlaws no longer hold up stagecoaches and rob banks, but Wyoming is still alive with the spirit of the Wild West. To be specific, about 5,000 spirits of the Wild West. Herds of wild horses—descendants of animals turned loose or escaped from early Spanish explorers, settlers, ranchers, cavalry, prospectors, and Indian tribes—still roam the state's public lands.

But these horses cannot be left to themselves. With no real natural predators or diseases, wild horses, if left unchecked, would dominate the state's open range. Wildlife and livestock would both suffer. To prevent this from happening, the Bureau of Land Management rounds up some of the mustangs every few years and sells them. But how do you efficiently round up animals scattered across hundreds of thousands of acres? Why, by helicopter, of course! It's certainly not how it was done in the Wild West, but we bet Buffalo Bill himself would have approved if helicopters had been around in his day. There are few sights as incongruous as watching a herd of horses run across the open prairie chased by a helicopter.

If you can't catch a helicopter roundup, the next best thing is to check in with the Pryor Mountain Mustang Herd. Alone among Wyoming's wild horses, the Pryor Mountain herd, north of Lovell, retains many of the markings of the Spanish mustang. This herd is considered so unique, in fact, that it inspired the creation of the country's first wild-horse preserve.

Want to do more than look at wild horses? If you've got the space, you can take one home with you. Anyone of legal age who can provide proper care and facilities for a horse can adopt one for a mere $125. Now that's a unique souvenir! For more information about the Pryor Mountain Mustang Herd, call (406) 896–5000.

TOUGH ON CRIME AS WELL AS JUST PLAIN TOUGH

In the late 1880s Newcastle's first mayor proposed shipping twenty of the biggest troublemakers out of town. A hooligan-supporter responded by shooting him. Like most Wyomingites of the time, however, the mayor was tough. He survived and went on to serve as a Wyoming congressman in Washington, D.C., for twenty-six years . . . with the bullet still lodged in him the entire time.

SEMANTICS If you want to play local here, be sure you say "Powder River" and not "the Powder River." For whatever reason, Powder River is one of the few rivers to have bucked tradition and is never preceded by "the."

Digging a Hole to China . . . or at Least to Oil
Newcastle

The fact that most oil wells are thousands of feet deep didn't deter a Newcastle-area rancher from trying his hand, and pick and shovel, at digging one of his own in 1966.

In an area so rich with oil, he didn't need to dig that far—a mere 24 feet down—before he struck black gold. The well is supposedly the world's only producing hand-dug oil well.

Today, more than forty years after that rancher tossed the first shovelful of dirt over his shoulder, the well is still going strong. To help you imagine what is going on underground, the Accidental Oil Company has also made a viewing-room oil well, an actual producing well that you can walk right into. They've also got what very well might be the world's most unique gift shop: It started its life as an oil tanker.

Cowboy Cry

Powder River Basin

Powder River Basin was the heart of Wyoming's Indian/soldier/cowboy country.

During the 1860s Indians and soldiers alike died in the Fetterman Fight, the Wagon Box Fight, and a battle on land that is now a Ranchester city park. Then, in the 1890s, cattlemen and homesteaders here fought one another in a bloody range war.

Powder River Basin is full of blood-soaked heroics and horror, but it wasn't until soldiers from seven western states found themselves gathered together on the Franco-Belgian border during World War II that Powder River became a battle cry. Patrolling this border far from home, the men of the 361st Infantry Regiment of the 91st Infantry Division adopted "Powder River, let 'er buck!" as its official battle cry. Nowadays, the cry is heard much closer to home: It is a favorite rallying call of the University of Wyoming Cowboys football team.

Stealing the Show

Ranchester

The 1904 St. Louis World's Fair had an Aeronautic Concourse, a 112-foot-diameter floral clock, an 80-foot papier-mâché whale, the Liberty Bell, the log cabin in which President Abraham Lincoln was born, and a 28-inch black-spotted Rocky Mountain trout caught on the Haley Ranch outside Ranchester. The titanic fish, caught in 1903, was mounted by a local taxidermist and, before making its way east to St. Louis to represent Wyoming, was exhibited at the Wyoming Industrial Convention to gaping mouths and disbelieving eyes. Despite its extreme size, the giant trout seems to have been misplaced since returning from St. Louis.

Try Not to Read Everything at Once
Recluse

The Campbell County Library might have dropped the Recluse Branch Library from its system a decade or so ago, but the locals have taken it upon themselves to keep their book cupboards stocked. Yes, that's right, the entire collection of the Recluse Library is housed in several wooden cupboards at one end of the Community Center.

When it was built in 1934—out of logs cut and hauled by locals—the Recluse Community Center was meant to be a multipurpose space. It wasn't until 1976, though, that "library" came to be included in the multiple purposes of the building. With funds secured through a bicentennial grant, the community center was able to build some book cupboards. With the cupboards in place, the Campbell County Library system was happy to supply about seventy-five books for a Recluse Branch Library.

However, this branch library was not only short on books but also a bit lacking in staff. In its final years librarian Pat Brose, who is based at the main branch of the Campbell County Library system 40-some miles away in Gillette, would travel to Recluse with a fresh supply of books about once a month. Pat eventually brought the number of books in the Recluse collection up to about 300. While Pat's appearance was always welcome, she didn't have to be present for the library to open. On the days when Pat was back in Gillette at her home base, Recluse Library patrons interested in returning or checking out a book would call the secretary at Oedekoven Water and Hot Oil Service, which sits right next to the community center. The secretary would come over and unlock the cupboards.

When the Campbell County Library system announced its pullout from Recluse, resident bookworms put out a call for donations of reading materials. The response was overwhelming, and today the cupboards overflow with everything from Danielle Steele to more sets of encyclopedias than anyone could read in a lifetime. The community center now has more books than when it was still an official library. Other benefits of no longer being official include no due dates, late fines, or even checkout procedures.

With its collection continually growing—patrons seem to drop off more books than they check out—Recluse residents plan a major renovation of the community center and library. In the renovated building the library and archives will get an entire room. There's no news yet of what new purpose the old cupboards might be appropriated for.

THAT WASN'T SUPPOSED TO HAPPEN

And just in case you're wondering how Recluse got its name, it does have to do with being a recluse. When the first post office opened in the area, it was quite far from any of the ranches it served. The ranchers thought that only a recluse would want to be that far away from others. And so the reclusive post office eventually became Recluse the town.

Walk This Way

Shell

You might be able to step in the footprints of Hollywood's biggest stars, such as Douglas Fairbanks, Marilyn Monroe, Tom Hanks, and even Donald Duck, at Mann's Chinese Theatre in Los Angeles, but only in Shell, Wyoming, can you see the footsteps of some of history's biggest stars. The Red Gulch Dinosaur Tracksite has 167-million-year-old footprints from hundreds of dinosaurs. All of the tracks that have been identified so far belong to meat-eating bipeds (therapods).

Scientists used to think that Wyoming was completely underwater during the Middle Jurassic period, which was 160 to 180 million years ago. In 1997 local hikers debunked that theory when they discovered these tracks, which were later dated to the Middle Jurassic. As a result of these findings, scientists now theorize that much of Wyoming was indeed covered with water but that this area was the shoreline and beach, which were covered by a cementlike mud rather than soft, white sand. The dinosaurs didn't seem to mind the mud, though. And it is because they were doing their seaside frolicking in cementlike mud instead of soft sand that, 167 million years later, their footprints remain. The mud did eventually harden. Then, over tens of millions of years, the footprints were covered by layers of dirt. Over more tens of millions of years, the dirt eroded, and the footprints were eventually exposed.

To visit the Red Gulch Dinosaur Tracksite, take U.S. Highway 14 and go 4 miles west from Shell to the Red Gulch turnoff. Call (307) 347–5100 for more information.

She Let Her Fingers Do the Walking

Sheridan

It wasn't exactly fast phoning that brought the rock star Prince to Sheridan in 1986, but rather diligent dialing. Sheridan resident Lisa Barber was the 10,000th—the winning—caller to MTV's "Prince Under the Cherry Moon" contest. As the contest's winner, Lisa won the right to host the world premiere of Prince's movie, *Under the Cherry Moon,* in her town. The flick was screened at Sheridan's Centennial Theaters, and since he was already here, Prince played a concert afterward at the Sheridan Holiday Inn. As an extra treat, Prince even took Lisa out on a date before jetting off.

Even though the *Under the Cherry Moon* premiere was highly successful—the theater was packed, and it was undoubtedly the biggest social happening of the year—it didn't exactly inspire Hollywood to rush back to Sheridan. Not until fall 2006 did the town play host to another movie premiere. *Flicka,* starring Tim McGraw, Alison Lohman, and Maria Bello, was screened for eager audiences here the night before its big Tinseltown premiere. This time around it wasn't someone winning a contest that was behind the premiere but rather the fact that *Flicka* had been filmed in and around Sheridan. And while the movie *Wild Horses* didn't premiere here, area residents still talk about star Kenny Rogers being tossed through the front window of the town's iconic Mint Bar during the film's making. The window has since been replaced.

People's Politicians
Sheridan

The Greek comedic writer Aristophanes probably didn't have the Sheridan Municipal Cemetery in mind when he penned, "Under every stone lurks a politician," but the line works nonetheless. The Sheridan Municipal Cemetery isn't quite as chock-full of politicians and historical figures as Arlington National Cemetery, but odds are it is the final resting place of more political bigwigs than any other municipal cemetery in the country.

Sheridan's answer to Arlington National Cemetery.

Three members of the U.S. Congress—Henry Asa Coffeen (elected as a Democrat to the House of Representatives in 1892), William Henry Harrison (a Republican in the House of Representatives from 1927 to 1929 and the great-great-grandson of President William Henry Harrison and grandson of President Benjamin Harrison), and John B. Kendrick (a Democratic senator from 1917 until his death in 1933)—elected to lurk under (head)stones here, coffin-to-coffin with the people they represented.

The Sheridan Municipal Cemetery is at 1000 Ash Street.

LOVE AT FIRST SIGHT

William Jennings Bryan needed only a few minutes in Sheridan to determine that it was one of the most beautiful towns in the world. In fact, he was so immediately taken with Sheridan during his 1919 "visit" that he didn't even have to leave the train station to form his high opinion. But, despite being so impressed with the town, the politician and orator reboarded his train after a mere fifteen minutes here and continued on his journey, never to return to this "beautiful" town again.

Malicious Mice?
Sheridan

Lacking the fire codes, smoke detectors, sprinkler systems, and on-the-ball fire departments that are so common today, the late 1800s and early 1900s weren't good times for preventing and fighting fires. Once a fire started, any nearby buildings generally became toast. But really, could fire prevention and firefighting have been so bad off that mice were able to send a building up in flames?

In 1915 fire destroyed the Sheridan Commercial Building, home to the mercantile/hardware store Sheridan Commercial Company, on Broadway in downtown. Some theorized that the fire was caused by mice whose nest-building accidentally ignited a match. However the fire started, it grew to be a rager, burning so large and hot that it even warped the train tracks behind the store.

The store's owners didn't let the mice get the better of them, though. By the next year, a new store was built on the ashes of the old one. That second building is still standing and still home to the same store. The rumor is that their selection of mousetraps is unparalleled. The Sheridan Commercial Company is at 303 Broadway. Call (307) 672–2451 for store hours.

IT'S ALL IN A NAME?

Just down Broadway from the Sheridan Commercial Company is the Cady Building. In the early 1900s its third floor was home to the Cady Opera House. You might notice that today the building has no third floor. One night in 1906, perhaps jinxed by that evening's operatic production, *The Runaway Match*, the building was almost completely destroyed by a fire. Using many of the original stones, the Cady Building was quickly rebuilt. No more operas were held there, however.

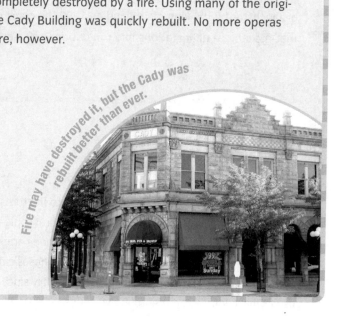

Fire may have destroyed it, but the Cady was rebuilt better than ever.

LAUGHABLE LAWSUIT

Talk about a frivolous lawsuit. In a case originally filed in federal district court in Wyoming, Robert Brewster, claiming to be a direct descendant of Plymouth Colony founder William Brewster, was looking for the U.S. government to restore some land to him. Brewster alleged that all land stretching north of Boulder, Colorado, to the Canadian border and from the Pacific to the Atlantic Ocean had been given to his ancestor by the king of England. In 1990 the court concluded that the statute of limitations had run out on Brewster's claim.

Mayo Clinic for Mounts
Sheridan

Dr. Ted Vlahos treats everything from cancer to fractures, neonates, and toothaches. He takes X-rays, performs arthroscopic surgery, and designs prosthetics to replace limbs that have been amputated. Every so often he even does embryo transfers. Dr. Vlahos is a modern-day country doctor through and through . . . especially since his patients usually have four legs rather than two. Since 1997 Dr. Vlahos and his team have given animals—mostly horses—access to pretty much the same type and level of medical care that are available to humans.

Horses used to be shot if they broke their leg, but Dr. Vlahos has proved that doesn't have to be the case. Take Lakota, who had a problem in the lower part of his foreleg that was bullet-worthy if anything was. But Dr. Vlahos went with A(mputation) before B(ullet). Lakota was very much alive, not to mention up and walking around, on a new custom prosthetic leg, only a few hours after Dr. Vlahos amputated his lower leg. Dr. Vlahos is one of the few animal surgeons who does prosthetics, and the Sheridan Equine Center is a pioneer in the field. In less extreme cases Dr. Vlahos can also fix broken bones with plain pins and screws. Even these are revolutionary when applied to horses, though.

BEGINNER'S LUCK

The year was 1905, and the Sheridan High School girls' basketball team was getting ready for their first-ever game. The girls, up against Buffalo High School, had no idea what to expect—only one team member had ever before played basketball. Whether that one experienced player scored all of Sheridan's points or whether her teammates picked up on the game very quickly has been lost to history. Either way, Sheridan won in a landslide: 16 to 3.

The Other Don King
Sheridan

Don King has made hand-carved leather saddles and belts for former presidents Ronald Reagan and Bill Clinton and the prince of Saudi Arabia, is one of the founding artisans of the National Cowboy and Western Heritage Museum (in Oklahoma City, Oklahoma, in case you're wondering), and has revolutionized cowboy ropes. King's Saddlery is today taking custom orders for delivery in 2010. Still, this Don King—Donald Lee King of Sheridan, Wyoming—is not the Don King that

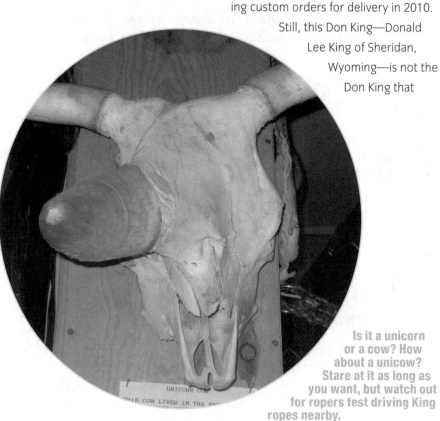

UNICORN CO[W]

[T]HIS COW LIVED IN THE PR...

Is it a unicorn or a cow? How about a unicow? Stare at it as long as you want, but watch out for ropers test driving King ropes nearby.

comes to mind when you first hear the name. That Don King, of course, would be the outspoken boxing promoter with vertical hair.

But the confusion of names doesn't bother Sheridan's Don King. After all, his rope and saddlery shop on Sheridan's main street makes and ships more ropes to more places around the world than anyone else; if they could, cowboys would line up to trade their firstborn for one of his custom saddles. Sure, you could wander into King's Saddlery to gape at the inventory of 30,000 coiled ropes—in both heading and heeling lengths and in more colors than a box of Crayola crayons—but your jaw will fall a lot farther when you enter the King Museum, containing his private collection of western memorabilia. (Whether you choose to gape at the ropes or the museum, which is just to the side of the rope racks, be on the watch for airborne ropes. Cowboys let fly different ropes at a dummy steer until they find one that feels just right.)

The King Museum, which opened in 1989, houses such treasures as a unicorn cow, a hat that once belonged to Gary Cooper, 550 antique and modern saddles (making it one of the largest private collections in the world), an original prairie wagon, Andy Warhol's concho belt, and John Wayne's very own leather breeches from the movie *Red River*. Don is happy to admit that part of the reason he wanted to open the museum was so he would have room to collect even more.

But let's get back to that unicorn cow. To explain: Here in the West, people don't often mess with fancy words and flowery descriptions. The "unicorn cow" is just what you would guess: a cow that looks like a unicorn. Or at least whose head does. This unfortunate guy was born with one of his horns coming straight out of his forehead. The supporting cast in the museum's festival of taxidermy includes the skulls of a pair of elk that died with their antlers so entangled, or embedded, in each other that they remain stuck together to this day.

THE ROYAL TREATMENT

If you shop at King's Saddlery, you're literally following in royal footsteps: During her 1984 visit to Sheridan—she checked in with old friends in Senator Malcolm Wallop's family—Queen Elizabeth II spent time browsing in this store, buying some bits for daughter Anne and accepting a gift of a hand-carved leather wastebasket/magazine holder from Don King himself. But because Don hadn't yet opened his museum, she didn't get to encounter the unicorn cow or John Wayne's breeches.

White Gables

Sheridan

Sheridan isn't really known for its raging floodwaters, but one of the theories behind the interesting architecture of the historic Sheridan Inn is that, if a monumental flood ever were to strike, the inn would just flip over and float merrily along, generally unharmed, until the floodwaters receded. The historic record shows that architect Thomas Kimball actually designed the three-story, sixty-nine-gabled inn—it doesn't take too much imagination to see it rolling over and sailing away—based on a Scottish castle he saw and liked, but who's to say that that Scottish castle wasn't designed for the flip-and-float maneuver?

The inn's unique architecture didn't keep guests away, though. The inn was the fanciest building between Chicago and San Francisco and the only building in Sheridan with electric lights when it was finished in 1893 (which, totally coincidentally, happened to be the same year the U.S. Supreme Court legally declared the tomato a vegetable). It has hosted everyone from Ernest Hemingway to President Herbert Hoover, Will Rogers, Thomas Dewey, Wendell Wilkie, Bob Hope, and a prima ballerina of the Russian Ballet Company.

Hemingway actually started writing *A Farewell to Arms* while staying here, but he quickly left because he found the place too boisterous for him to concentrate on his craft (remember, this is the man who did much of his writing in the Spanish town famous for its running of the bulls!). It's no wonder Ernie found it disruptive: Buffalo Bill, who owned

This porch is peaceful now.

the business for many years, used to have target practice from the rocking chairs on the front porch, and wannabe performers in his Wild West show auditioned out front (though not necessarily while Bill was having target practice). Local cowboys would have semiregular horse races starting at and finishing *in* the Inn: The winner would ride his horse right into the inn's bar and buy a round for everyone.

The rowdiness didn't scare everyone away, though. One woman loved the place so much that her dying wish was to have her ashes buried here. Miss Kate Arnold first came to the Sheridan Inn in 1901 as a fresh-faced twenty-two-year-old looking for a job. She started at the inn as a seamstress and, over the next sixty-four years, did everything from desk clerking to housekeeping, hostessing, and babysitting. Miss Kate finally moved out of the inn in 1965 when a new owner was planning to tear it down (this despite its being recently showcased in *Ripley's Believe It Or Not* for its many gables). A local advocacy group kept the demolition from happening, however, and, upon Miss Kate's death in 1968, she was moved back to the inn. Her ashes are buried in the wall of her favorite third-floor room . . . or first-floor room if the inn ever does manage to flip over.

The Sheridan Inn hasn't been open to overnight guests since 1965, but a renovation of the guest rooms is planned. In the meantime, the inn's restaurant is open, and the inn itself can be toured. Keep your eyes and ears out for Miss Kate's ghost.

The Sheridan Inn is at 856 Broadway. For more information call (307) 674–5440.

PERHAPS CRAZY HORSE SLEPT HERE?

Native-American warrior Crazy Horse spent 80 percent of his adult life within 100 miles of Sheridan.

It's Not Your Imagination
Sheridan

The western blockbuster *The Horse Whisperer* might have been filmed in Montana by a director who spends a lot of time in Utah, but the inspiration behind the main character lies right here in Sheridan. Area horse trainer extraordinaire Buck Brannaman spent months with Robert Redford helping prepare the actor/director to bring the horse-whispering main character Tom Booker to life. Brannaman was so inspirational in fact—not that he would ever admit this himself—that the movie's costumer pretty much dressed Tom Booker exactly as Brannaman dresses, right down to the Rockmount shirts and Filson coats. So, if you see someone who looks, and acts, a lot like Robert Redford's Horse Whisperer character walking down Main Street, you're not imagining things.

Buck Brannaman has spent more than twenty years—starting when he was just a teenager—working with horses and their owners. When not jetting around the country—so far he's done clinics in more than thirty states, "whispering" to more than 1,000 horses a year—Buck has found time enough to practice his trick roping skills. He holds two roping titles in the *Guinness Book of World Records*. Trick roping and traveling aside, Buck sets aside much of the month of February to hang at home. His ranch, just outside Sheridan, has an arena where he does horse-help sessions that are open to the public. From November through March Buck's arena is also home to cowboy competitions open to men, women, and children.

For more information call Sheridan Travel and Tourism at (307) 673–7120 or visit www.sheridanwyoming.org.

It's All in the Name

Sundance

If my given name were plain old Harry Longabaugh, I might go looking for a slightly more exciting moniker—although I probably wouldn't rename myself in quite the same manner that one particular Harry Longabaugh did in the late 1800s. Barely through his teenage years, this Harry Longabaugh found himself working as a ranch hand at the VVV Ranch outside of Sundance, Wyoming. He evidently also found himself very interested in a light gray horse belonging to one of his fellow ranch hands, Alonzo Craven.

One day in 1897 when Alonzo was looking the other way, Harry, a native of Pennsylvania, stole the horse, along with the saddle and gun on its back. He fled to Miles City, Montana, with his booty—estimated to be worth about $80—but was caught a few months later and brought back to Sundance. He was tried and convicted of three counts of grand larceny (the horse, the saddle, and the gun were each one count).

Because of his young age, Harry got out of hard labor at the state penitentiary and was allowed to serve out his eighteen months right here in Sundance. The town was so unaccustomed to having lawbreakers around that Harry had the jail all to himself. When he was released, Harry, despite having traded up to the more exciting and original name

"Sundance Kid," left town and never returned. That was just fine with the good folks of Sundance, though; the Kid's antics—robbing trains and banks with Butch Cassidy and other members of the Hole-in-the-Wall Gang—weren't exactly of the kind any town wanted around.

Nowadays, Sundance the town celebrates Sundance the Kid. There's a bronze statue of him downtown, and the Crook County Museum proudly displays the original courtroom furniture from the Kid's 1897 trial. You're not allowed to sit in the same wooden chair the Kid sat in as his "guilty" verdict was read, but the museum hopes you'll stop by to look at it. The Crook County Museum is in the Crook County Courthouse in downtown Sundance. For hours and other information call (307) 283–3666.

Ten Sleeps in the Middle of Nowhere
Ten Sleep

Tucked into the western flanks of the Bighorn Mountains, Ten Sleep is isolated even today. Back when it was named Ten Sleep, however, it was even more isolated. You see, Ten Sleep is named for the Native American method of reckoning time and measuring distance—by the number of days, or "sleeps," it takes to get there. Ten Sleep was a full ten sleeps away from pretty much everything—Yellowstone National Park; the closest major Sioux camp, on the North Platte River outside the present-day city of Casper; and the Indian agency at Stillwater, Montana. Good thing the name Ten Sleep was established before modern methods of travel came about: One Hour—the driving distance by car from Ten Sleep to Buffalo, the nearest major town—doesn't sound nearly so good.

FINE DRINKING

Aqua Vista bottled water is sold throughout the northern Rocky Mountains, but you can enjoy it for free in Ten Sleep. Aqua Vista water actually comes from Ten Sleep's artesian wells. Drink up!

It Must Be Something in the Water
Ucross

Ucross, named after the original brand of the Pratt & Ferris Cattle Company, has a population of only twenty-five, yet it can claim Pulitzer Prize–winner Annie Proulx, National Book Award Honorees Ha Jin and Bob Shacochis, MacArthur Fellow Colson Whitehead, and Tony Award–winning playwright Craig Lucas as residents. Well, part-time residents. Each of these big-time creative types has spent time in residence at the Ucross Foundation, one of the world's foremost working retreats for artists and writers. About sixty-five artists and writers spend time here annually. Since accepting its first artists-in-residence in 1983, Ucross Foundation has hosted more than 1,300 artists and writers from all fifty states and twenty foreign countries. That's fifty times as many artists as year-round residents.

If you're going to be in the area, make sure to call the foundation to see if any of its resident writers or artists will be doing shows or readings. Performances are held at both the foundation and at area bookstores and galleries. Wyoming might have only one Barnes and Noble (about five hours from Ucross), a scarcity of concert halls, and no modern art museums, but no one around here seems to mind. You can walk into a Buffalo bookstore and hear Annie Proulx read something from the book she's currently working on or see original "sunprints" by New York–based artist Lindy Smith at the Ucross Foundation Art Galley, which holds four contemporary exhibitions per year.

Soak up some of the creative juices of the Ucross Foundation's fellows at 30 Big Red Lane. Call (307) 737–2291 for more information.

More literary greats have slept here than anywhere else.

A LIST IT'S GOOD TO BE AT THE BOTTOM OF

In 1996 Wyoming was ranked as forty-third on a list of most annoying states by *Spy* magazine. Texas was named the most annoying (first). New Jersey was least annoying (fiftieth).

Dude, It Was the Birth of an Industry!
Wolf

The oldest dude ranch in the world is in Wyoming, but another, different dude ranch claims the honor of being Wyoming's oldest. Got that? Eaton's Ranch launched the dude-ranching industry when it welcomed its first dudes, vacationers interested in playing cowboy, in 1879. The Eatons didn't mean to start a business—it was initially just friends visiting from the East who came out—but these friends, realizing that their extended stays were costly for their hosts, prevailed upon the family to charge for room and board. With cattle prices collapsing and blizzards decimating their herds, the Eatons eventually accepted. With the Eaton Ranch as a model, Crossed Sabers Ranch opened more than a decade later, in 1898. Crossed Sabers, however, calls itself Wyoming's oldest dude ranch, and Eaton's Ranch knows it is right . . . that's because Eaton's is an import.

Eaton's, established by brothers Howard, Willis, and Alden Eaton, initially welcomed guests near Medora, in the Dakota Territory. The brothers took their time in realizing that the mountains around Wolf Creek would provide better scenery for their saddled-up guests than the plains around Medora. In 1904, a full six years after Crossed Sabers opened in the national forest outside of Cody, the Eaton boys pulled up stakes in Medora and headed to Wolf Creek, where the 7,000-acre ranch still welcomes guests today. In a state where cows outnumber people by a factor of nearly three, there is plenty of room for both ranches, though . . . and several dozen much newer additions.

Eaton's Ranch is off County Road 89, about twenty-five minutes from downtown Sheridan. For more information call (307) 655–9285 or visit www.eatonsranch.com.

Moving On Up to the East Side . . . and Then Back West
Worland

It used to be Worland was on the western shore of the Bighorn River. Its general store, a few houses, a dance hall, two saloons, the school, and an office building were perfectly content and settled there by the early twentieth century. But then the railroad came to town. And the railroad had it in its head that it was going to put the tracks and depot on the eastern side of the Bighorn River. Nothing the town said or did could convince the railroad to build on the western shore.

As Worlanders saw it, they were left with but one choice: to move the town. Thankfully, as often happened—and still occasionally happens—the winter of 1905–1906

Worland's buildings weren't meant to be mobile, but they still manage to move around a lot.

was a harsh one. The town was covered in snow, and the river completely froze over. Nowadays, there are all sorts of ways to move buildings, but back then there were no mechanical cranes, jacks, or the like. The only horsepower was real horse power. The men of Worland carefully raised each building . . . and then just slid them across the frozen river. Voilà! Thanks to Wyoming's hard winters, Worland and the train were now on the same side of the river.

Today, there is one house known to have been among those moved from west to east . . . and it has been moved *back* to the west side. In 1982, when no one was living in it, the Widow Ludlow's house was taken back west. This time, however, the two-story structure was loaded onto the back of a truck, although that didn't necessarily make the moving easier: In the years since the first move, power lines had been invented. One Worland lawyer who helped with the move says he thinks the house might have hit a line or two.

If you want to see what may be one of the most-traveled homes in the state, take Fifteen Mile Road off Highway 433. Widow Ludlow's house sits on the right side, about ½ mile down the road.

Where's the Water?
Worland

You wouldn't expect to find whales in Wyoming, but Worland claims no fewer than three. Sort of. The three 15- to 20-foot whale-shaped formations rising out of the desert landscape a few miles outside of town might very well be whale fossils . . . or they could be the result of tens of thousands of years of geology at work. Not surprisingly, the whale hypothesis is more popular among locals. I'm going to run with that.

Hundreds of millions of years ago, Wyoming was a tropical, oceanside paradise. Well, to be more precise, it was an ocean paradise, buried hundreds of feet beneath water. The water gradually receded, and these colossal triplets somehow got stuck on one of Wyoming's newly exposed beaches and died. That's the theory at least. Over the course of an indeterminate number of years, sand and rock built up around the whales' bodies. Their skeletons stayed mostly intact while their body cavities were filled in. Over the next tens of millions of years, they fossilized, and the sand that had built up around them eventually eroded, leaving the whales swimming in a sea of sage.

"This scenario isn't totally and completely without precedent, but it is quite rare," says local Bureau of Land Management geologist Mike Bies. "I don't want to tell anyone they're wrong when they say these are whales, though. Whales are a more interesting and imaginative explanation than the geologic one."

For directions to the whales, stop by the Bureau of Land Management's Worland Field Office at 101 South Twenty-third Street or call (307) 347–5100.

Sea World and Shamu have nothing on Wyoming.

INDEX

INDEX

INDEX

INDEX

INDEX

About the Author

Dina Mishev has been living and writing in Jackson Hole, Wyoming, since 1997. A graduate of Northwestern University with degrees in Math and Economics, Dina moved to Wyoming for a year immediately following college. The plan was to learn how to ski and then return to law school on the East Coast the following fall. The latter part of that plan was thrown out the window within two weeks of her arrival in Jackson. The former part remains a work in progress. When snow is in short supply, Dina races her road bike, climbs, hikes, explores her adopted state via motorcycle, and makes cookie dough.

Dina's writing career stared shortly after her arrival in Wyoming when the *Jackson Hole News* entrusted her to write a bi-weekly column about twenty-something life in the valley. As she had no real writing clips (math majors rarely do), her "application" included photocopied pages from her journal. Five years later Dina was interning and writing for *Outside* magazine. Today she writes about travel, sports, adventure, gear, art, people, and lifestyle topics for *Outside, National Geographic Adventure, the Chicago Tribune, Cooking Light, NWA World Traveler, United Hemispheres, Wyoming Tourism, Arizona Tourism,* and *Mobil Travel Guide.* Assignments have taken her from spas in Africa to granite cliffs in Tasmania. Dina also does freelance editing and writes profiles, press releases, and advertorial copy for business clients. This is her first book.